A SHORT AN METHOD

CW01510344

WHICH ALL CAN PRACTICE WITH THE GREATEST FACILITY, AND ARRIVE IN A SHORT TIME, BY ITS MEANS, AT A HIGH DEGREE OF PERFECTION.

BY

MADAME GUYON.

EDITED BY JAMES W. METCALF

"Walk before me and be thou perfect."—Gen. xvii. 1.

NEW YORK:
PUBLISHED BY M. W. DODD,
BRICK CHURCH CHAPEL, CITY HALL SQUARE
1853

This title was originally part of a larger work entitled *Spiritual Progress: or Instructions in the Divine Life of the Soul From the French of Fenelon and Madame Guyon* edited by James W. Metcalf. Available from CrossReach Publications in eBook and Paperback editions.

CROSSREACH
PUBLICATIONS

Hope. Inspiration. Trust.

WE'RE SOCIAL! FOLLOW US FOR NEW TITLES AND DEALS:
FACEBOOK.COM/CROSSREACHPUBLICATIONS
TWITTER HANDLE: @CROSSREACHPUB

AVAILABLE IN PAPERBACK AND EBOOK EDITIONS
PLEASE GO ONLINE FOR MORE GREAT TITLES
AVAILABLE THROUGH CROSSREACH PUBLICATIONS.
AND IF YOU ENJOYED THIS BOOK PLEASE CONSIDER LEAVING A
REVIEW ON AMAZON. THAT HELPS US OUT A LOT. THANKS.

CONTENTS

THE AUTHOR'S PREFACE.

This little treatise, conceived in great simplicity, was not originally intended for publication. It was written for a few individuals, who were desirous of loving God with all their heart. Many, however, because of the profit they received in reading the manuscript, wished to obtain copies, and, on this account alone, it was committed to the press.

It still remains in its original simplicity. It contains no censure on the various divine leadings of others; on the contrary, it enforces the received teachings. The whole is submitted to the judgment of the learned and experienced; requesting them, however, not to stop at the surface, but to enter into the main design of the author, which is to *induce the whole world to love God, and to serve Him with comfort and success,* in a simple and easy manner, adapted to those *little ones* who are unqualified for learned and deep researches, but who earnestly *desire to be truly devoted to God.*

An unprejudiced reader will find, hidden under the most common expressions, a secret unction, which will excite him to seek after that happiness which all should wish to enjoy.

In asserting that perfection is easily attained, the word *facility,* is used; because God is, indeed found with facility, *when we seek Him within ourselves.* But some, perhaps, may urge that passage in St. John *"Ye shall seek me, and shall not find me,"* (vii. 34); this apparent difficulty, however, is removed by another passage, where He, who cannot contradict himself, has said to all, *"Seek and ye shall find,"* (Matt. vii. 7). It is true, indeed, that he who would seek God, seeks Him where He is not; and, therefore, it is added, *"Ye shall die in your sins."* But he, who will take some trouble to seek God in his own heart, and sincerely forsake his sin, that he may draw near unto Him, shall infallibly find Him.

A life of *piety* appears so frightful to many, and *prayer* of such difficult attainment, that they are discouraged from taking a single step towards it. But as the apprehended difficulty of an undertaking often causes despair of succeeding and reluctance in commencing, so its desirableness, and the idea that it is easy to accomplish, induce us to enter upon its pursuit with pleasure, and to pursue it with vigor. The advantages and *facility* of this way are therefore set forth in the following treatise.

O were we once persuaded of the goodness of God toward his poor creatures, and of his desire to communicate Himself to them, we should not create ideal monsters, nor so easily despair of obtaining that good which He is so earnest to bestow: *"He that spared not his own Son, but delivered him up for us all; how shall He not, with him, also freely give us all things?"* (Rom. viii. 32). It needs only a little courage and perseverance; we have enough of both in our temporal concerns, but none at all in the one thing needful, (Luke x. 42).

If any think that God is not easily to be found in this way, let them not on my testimony alter their minds, but let them try it, and their own experience will convince them, that the reality far exceeds all my representations of it.

Beloved reader, pursue this little tract with a sincere and candid spirit, in lowliness of mind, and not with an inclination to criticize, and you will not fail to reap profit from it. It was written with a desire that you might *wholly devote yourself to God;* receive it then with a like desire: for it has no other design than to invite the simple and the child-like to approach their father, who delights in the humble confidence of his children, and is greatly grieved at their distrust. With a sincere desire, therefore, for your salvation, seek nothing from the unpretending method here proposed, but the love of God, and you shall assuredly obtain it.

Without setting up our opinions above those of others, we mean only with sincerity to declare, from our own experience and the experience of others, the happy effects produced by thus simply following after the Lord.

As this treatise was intended only to instruct in prayer, nothing is said of many things which we esteem, because they do not immediately relate to our main subject. It is, however, beyond a doubt, that nothing will be found herein to offend, provided it be read in the spirit with which it was written. And it is still more certain, that those who in right earnest make trial of the way, will find we have written the truth.

It is Thou alone, O holy Jesus, who lovest simplicity and innocence, *and whose delight is to dwell with the children of men,"* (Prov. viii. 31), with those who are, indeed, willing to become *"little children,"* (Matt. xviii. 3); it is Thou alone, who canst render this little work of any value, by imprinting it on the heart, and leading those who read it to seek Thee within themselves, where Thou reposest as in the manger, waiting to receive proofs of their love, and to give them testimony of thine. They lose these advantages by their own fault. But it belongeth unto thee, O child Almighty! uncreated Love! silent and all-containing Word! to make thyself loved, enjoyed and understood. Thou canst do it; and I know Thou wilt do it by this little work, which belongeth entirely to Thee, proceedeth wholly from Thee, and tendeth only to Thee!

CHAPTER I.

Introduction. That all are called to prayer, and by the aid of ordinary grace may put up the prayer of the heart, which is the great means of salvation, and which can be offered at all times, and by the most uninstructed.

All are capable of prayer, and it is a dreadful misfortune that almost all the world have conceived the idea that they are not called to prayer. We are all called to prayer, as we are all called to salvation.

Prayer is nothing but the *application of the heart to God,* and the internal exercise of love. St. Paul has enjoined us to *"pray without ceasing;"* (1 Thess. v. 17,) and our Lord bids us watch and pray, (Mark xiii. 33, 37): all therefore may, and all ought to practise prayer. I grant that meditation is attainable but by few, for few are capable of it; and therefore, my beloved brethren who are athirst for salvation, meditative prayer is not the prayer which

God requires of you, nor which we would recommend.

2. Let all pray: you should live by prayer, as you should live by love. *"I counsel you to buy of me gold tried in the fire, that ye may be rich."* (Rev. iii. 18.) This is very easily obtained, much more easily than you can conceive.

Come all ye that are athirst to the living waters, nor lose your precious moments in hewing our cisterns that will hold no water. (John vii. 37; Jer. ii. 13.) Come ye famishing souls, who find nought to satisfy you; come, and ye shall be filled! Come, ye poor afflicted ones, bending beneath your load of wretchedness and pain, and ye shall be consoled! Come, ye sick, to your physician, and be not fearful of approaching him because ye are filled with diseases; show them, and they shall be healed!

Children, draw near to your Father, and he will embrace you in the arms of love! Come ye poor, stray, wandering sheep, return to your Shepherd! Come, sinners, to your Saviour! Come ye dull, ignorant, and illiterate, ye who think yourselves the most incapable of prayer! ye are more peculiarly called and adapted thereto. Let all without exception come, for Jesus Christ hath called ALL.

Yet let not those come who are without a heart; they are excused; for there must be a heart before there can be love. But who is without a heart? O come, then, give this heart to God; and here learn how to make the donation.

3. All who are desirous of prayer, may easily pray, enabled by those ordinary graces and gifts of the Holy Spirit which are common to all men.

Prayer is the key to perfection, and the sovereign good; it is the means of delivering us from every vice, and obtaining us every virtue; for the one great means of becoming perfect, is to walk in the presence of God. He himself hath said, *"Walk before me, and be thou perfect."* (Gen. xvii. 1.) It is by prayer alone that we are brought into his presence, and maintained in it without interruption.

4. You must, then, learn a species of prayer which may be exercised at all times; which does not obstruct outward employments; which may be equally practised by princes, kings, prelates, priests and magistrates, soldiers and children, tradesmen, laborers, women, and sick persons; it is not the prayer of the head, but of the heart.

It is not a prayer of the understanding alone, for the mind of man is so limited in its operations that it can have but one object at a time; but it is the prayer of the heart which is not interrupted by the exercises of reason. Nothing can interrupt this prayer but disordered affections; and when once we have enjoyed God, and the sweetness of his love, we shall find it impossible to relish aught but himself.

5. Nothing is so easily obtained as the possession and enjoyment of God. He is more present to us than we are to ourselves. He is more desirous of giving Himself to us than we are to possess Him; we only need to know how to seek Him, and the way is easier and more natural to us than breathing.

Ah! ye who think yourselves so dull and fit for nothing, by prayer you may live on God himself with less difficulty or interruption that you live on the vital air. Will it not then be highly sinful to neglect prayer? But doubtless you will not, when you have learnt the method, which is the easiest in the world.

CHAPTER II.

1. First degree of prayer, practised in two ways; one by reading and meditation, the other by meditation alone.

2, 3. Rules and methods of meditation.

4. Remedies for its difficulties.

There are two ways of introducing some important practical or speculative truth, always preferring the practical, and proceeding thus: whatever truth you have chosen, read only a small portion of it, endeavoring to taste and digest it, to extract the essence and substance of it, and proceed no farther while any savor or relish remains in the passage: then take up your book again, and proceed as before, seldom reading more than half a page at a time.

It is not the quantity that is read, but the manner of reading, that yields us profit. Those who read fast, reap no more advantage, than a bee would by only skimming over the surface of the flower, instead of waiting to penetrate into it, and extract its sweets. Much reading is rather for scholastic subjects, than divine truths; to receive profit from spiritual books, we must read as I have described; and I am certain that if that method were pursued, we should become gradually habituated to pray by our reading, and more fully disposed for its exercise.

2. Meditation, which is the other method, is to be practised at an appropriated season, and not in the

time of reading. I believe that the best manner of meditating is as follows:

When by an act of lively faith, you are placed in the presence of God, read some truth wherein there is substance; pause gently thereon, not to employ the reason, but merely to fix the mind; observing that the principal exercise should ever be the presence of God, and that the subject, therefore, should rather serve to stay the mind, than exercise it in reasoning.

Then let a *lively faith in God immediately present in our inmost souls,* produce an eager sinking into ourselves, restraining all our senses from wandering abroad: this serves to extricate us, in the first instance, from numerous distraints, to remove us far from external objects, and to bring us nigh to God, who is only to be found in our inmost centre, which is the *Holy of Holies* wherein he dwells. He has even promised to come and make his abode with him that doeth his will. (John xiv. 23.) St. Augustine blames himself for the time he lost in not having sought God, from the first, in this manner of prayer.

3. When we are thus fully entered into ourselves, and warmly penetrated throughout with a lively sense of the Divine presence; when the senses are

all recollected, and withdrawn from the circumference to the centre, and the soul is sweetly and silently employed on the truths we have read, not in reasoning, but in feeding thereon, and animating the will by affection, rather than fatiguing the understanding by study; when, I say, the affections are in this state, (which, however difficult it may appear at first, is, as I shall hereafter show, easily attainable,) we must allow them *sweetly to repose,* and, as it were, *swallow* what they have tasted.

For as a person may enjoy the flavor of the finest viands in mastication, yet receive no nourishment from them, if he does not cease the action and swallow the food; so when our affections are enkindled, if we endeavor to stir them up yet more, we extinguish the flame, and the soul is deprived of its nourishment. We should, therefore, in a *repose of love,* full of respect and confidence, swallow the blessed food we have received. This method is highly necessary, and will advance the soul more in a short time, than any other in years.

4. But as I have said that our direct and principal exercise should consist *in the contemplation of the Divine presence,* we should be exceedingly diligent in *recalling our dissipated senses,* as the most easy method of overcoming distractions; for a direct

contest only serves to irritate and augment them; whereas, by sinking within, under a view by faith, of a present God, and simply recollecting ourselves, we wage insensibly very successful, though indirect war with them.

It is proper here to caution beginners against wandering from truth to truth, and from subject to subject; the right way to penetrate every divine truth, to enjoy its full relish, and to imprint it on the heart, is to dwell upon it whilst its savor continues.

Though recollection is *difficult* in the beginning, from the habit the soul has acquired of being always abroad, yet, when by the violence it has done itself, it becomes a little accustomed to it, the process is soon render perfectly easy; and this partly from the force of habit, and partly because God, whose one will towards his creatures is to communicate himself to them, imparts abundant grace, and an experimental enjoyment of his presence, which very much facilitate it.

CHAPTER III.

1. Method of meditative prayer for those who cannot read;

2, 3. Applied to the Lord's Prayer and to some of the attributes of God.

4. Transition from the first to the second degree of prayer.

Those who cannot read books, are not, on that account, excluded from prayer. The great book which teaches all things, and which is written all over, within and without, is Jesus Christ himself.

The method they should practice is this: they should first learn this fundamental truth, that *"the kingdom of God is within them,"* (Luke xvii. 21,) and that it must be sought there only.

It is as incumbent on the clergy to instruct their parishioners in prayer, as in their catechism. It is true they tell them the end of their creation; but they do not give them sufficient instructions how they may attain it.

They should be taught to begin by an act of profound adoration and annihilation before God, and closing the corporeal eyes, endeavor to open those of the soul; they should then collect themselves inwardly, and by a lively faith in God, as dwelling within them, pierce into the divine presence; not suffering the senses to wander abroad, but holding them as much as may be in subjection.

2. They should then repeat the Lord's prayer in their native tongue; pondering a little upon the meaning of the words, and the infinite willingness of that God who dwells within them to become, indeed, "their father." In this state let them pour out their wants before him; and when they have pronounced the word, "father," remain a few moments in a reverential silence, waiting to have the will of this their heavenly Father made manifest to them.

Again, the Christian, beholding himself in the state of a feeble child, soiled and sorely bruised by repeated falls, destitute of strength to stand, or of power to cleanse himself, should lay his deplorable situation open to his Father's view in humble confusion; occasionally intermingling a word or two of love and grief, and then again sinking into silence before Him. Then, continuing the Lord's prayer, let him beseech this King of Glory to reign in him, abandoning himself to God, that He may do it, and acknowledging his right to rule over him.

If they feel an inclination to peace and silence, let them not continue the words of the prayer so long as this sensation holds; and when it subsides, let them go on with the second petition, *"thy will be done on earth as it is in heaven!"* upon which let these humble supplicants beseech God to accomplish in them, and by them, all his will, and let them surrender their hearts and freedom into his hands, to be disposed of as He pleases. When they find that the will should be employed in loving, they will desire to love, and will implore Him for his love; but all this will take place sweetly and peacefully: and so of the rest of the prayer, in which the clergy may instruct them.

But they should not burthen themselves with frequent repetitions of set forms, or studied prayers; for the Lord's prayer once repeated as I have just described, will produce abundant fruit.

3. At other times, they may place themselves as sheep before their Shepherd, looking up to Him for their true food: O divine Shepherd, Thou feedest thy flock with Thyself, and art indeed their daily bread. They may also represent to him the necessities of their families: but let all be done from this principal and one great view of faith, that God is within them.

All our imaginations of God amount to nothing; a lively faith in his presence is sufficient. For we must not form any image of the Deity, though we may of Jesus Christ, beholding him in his birth, or his crucifixion, or in some other state or mystery, provided the soul always seeks Him in its own centre.

On other occasions, we may look to him as a physician, and present for his healing virtue all our maladies; but always without perturbation, and with pauses from time to time, that the silence, being mingled with action, may be gradually extended, and our own exertion lessened; till at length, by continually yielding to God's operations, He gains the complete ascendancy, as shall be hereafter explained.

4. When the divine presence is granted us, and we gradually begin to relish silence and repose, *this experimental enjoyment of the presence of God* introduces the soul into the second degree of prayer, which, by proceeding in the manner I have described, is attainable as well by the illiterate as by the learned; some privileged souls, indeed, are favored with it even from the beginning.

CHAPTER IV.

1. Second degree of prayer, called here "The prayer of simplicity." At what time we reach it.

2. How to offer and continue it.

3. Requisites to offering it acceptably.

Some call the second degree of prayer *Contemplation, The prayer of faith and stillness,* and others call it *The prayer of simplicity.* I shall here use this latter appellation, as being more just than that of contemplation, which implies a more advanced state than that I am now treating of.

When the soul has been for some time exercised in the way I have mentioned, it gradually finds that it is enabled to approach God with facility; that recollection is attended with much less difficulty, and that prayer becomes easy, sweet, and delightful: it recognizes that this is the true way of finding God, and feels that *" his name is as ointment poured forth."* (Cant. i. 3.) The method must now be altered, and that which I describe must be pursued with courage and fidelity, without being disturbed at the difficulties we may encounter in the way.

2. First, as soon as the soul by faith places itself in the presence of God, and becomes recollected before Him, let it remain thus for a little time in respectful silence.

But if, at the beginning, in forming the act of faith, it feels some little pleasing sense of the Divine presence, let it remain there without being troubled for a subject, and proceed no farther, but carefully cherish this sensation while it continues. When it abates, it may excite the will by some tender affection; and if, by the first moving thereof, it finds itself reinstated in sweet peace, let it there remain; the fire must be gently fanned, but as soon as it is kindled, we must cease our efforts, lest we extinguish it by our activity.

3. I would warmly recommend to all, never to finish prayer without remaining some little time afterward in a respectful silence. It is also of the greatest importance for the soul to go to prayer with courage, and to bring with it such a pure and disinterested love, as seeks nothing from God, but to please Him, and to do his will; for a servant who only proportions his diligence to his hope of reward, is unworthy of any recompense. Go then to prayer, not desiring to enjoy spiritual delights, but to be just as it pleases God; this will preserve your spirit tranquil in aridities as well as in consolation, and prevent your being surprised at the apparent repulses or absence of God.

CHAPTER V.

On various matters occurring in or belonging to the degree of prayer, that is to say,

1. On aridities; which are caused by deprivation of the sensible presence of God for an admirable end, and which are to be met by acts of solid and peaceful virtue of mind and soul.

2. Advantages of this course.

Though God has no other desire than to impart Himself to the loving soul that seeks Him, yet He frequently conceals Himself from it, that it may be roused from sloth, and impelled to seek Him with fidelity and love. But with what abundant goodness does He recompense the faithfulness of his beloved! And how often are these apparent withdrawings of Himself succeeded by the caresses of love!

At these seasons we are apt to believe that it proves our fidelity, and evinces a greater ardor of affection to seek Him by an exertion of our own strength and activity; or that such a course will induce Him the more speedily to revisit us. No, dear souls, believe me, this is not the best way in this degree of prayer; with patient love, with self-abasement and humiliation, with the reiterated breathings of an ardent but peaceful affection, and with silence full of veneration, you must await the return of the Beloved.

2. Thus only can you demonstrate that it is Himself alone, and his good pleasure, that you seek; and not the selfish delights of your own sensations in loving Him. Hence it is said (Eccles. ii. 2, 3): *"Be not impatient in the time of dryness and obscurity; suffer the suspensions and delays of the consolations of God; cleave unto him, and wait upon him patiently, that thy life may increase and be renewed."*

Be patient in prayer, though during your whole lifetime you should do nothing else than wait the return of the Beloved in a spirit of humiliation, abandonment, contentment, and resignation. Most excellent prayer! and it may be intermingled with the sighings of plaintive love! This conduct indeed is most pleasing to the heart of God, and will, above all others, compel his return.

CHAPTER VI.

1, 2. On the abandonment of self to God, its fruit, and its irrevocableness.

3. Its nature; God requires it.

4. Its practice.

Here we must begin to *abandon* and give up our whole existence to God, from the strong and positive conviction, that the occurrences of every moment result from his immediate will and permission, and are just such as our state requires. This conviction will make us content with everything; and cause us to regard all that happens, not from the side of the creature, but from that of God.

But, dearly beloved, whoever you are who sincerely wish to give yourselves up to God, I conjure you, that after having once made the donation, you take not yourselves back again; remember, a gift once presented, is no longer at the disposal of the giver.

2. *Abandonment* is a matter of the greatest importance in our progress; it is the key to the inner court; so that he who knows truly how to abandon himself, will soon become perfect. We must therefore continue steadfast and immovable therein, without listening to the voice of natural reason. Great faith produces great abandonment; we must confide in God, *"hoping against hope."* (Rom. iv. 18.)

3. *Abandonment* is the casting off all selfish care, that we may be altogether at the divine disposal.

All Christians are exhorted to abandonment; for it is said to all; *"Take no thought for the morrow; for your Heavenly Father knoweth that ye have need of all these things.* (Matt. vi. 32–34.) *"In all thy ways acknowledge him, and he shall direct thy paths."* (Prov. iii. 6.) *"Commit thy works unto the Lord and thy thoughts shall be established."* (Prov. xvi. 3.) *"Commit thy way unto the Lord; trust also in Him and He will bring it to pass."* (Psalm xxxvii. 5.)

Our abandonment, then, should be, both in respect to external and internal things, an absolute giving up of all our concerns into the hands of God, forgetting ourselves and thinking only of Him; by which the heart will remain always disengaged, free, and at peace.

4. It is practised by continually losing our own will in the will of God; renouncing every private inclination as soon as it arises, however good it may appear, that we may stand in indifference with respect to ourselves, and only will what God has willed from all eternity; resigning ourselves in all things, whether for soul or body, for time or eternity; forgetting the past, leaving the future to Providence, and devoting the present to God; satisfied with the present moment, which brings with it God's eternal order in reference to us, and

is as infallible a declaration of his will, as it is inevitable and common to all; attributing nothing that befalls us to the creature, but regarding all things in God, and looking upon all, excepting only our sins, as infallibly proceeding from Him.

Surrender yourselves then to be led and disposed of just as God pleases, with respect both to your outward and inward state.

CHAPTER VII.

1. On suffering: that it should be accepted from the hand of God.

2. Its use and profit.

3. Its practice.

Be patient under all the sufferings God sends; if your love to Him be pure, you will not seek Him less on Calvary, than on Tabor; and surely, He should be as much loved on that as on this, since it was on Calvary that he made the greatest display of love.

Be not like those who give themselves to Him at one season, only to withdraw from Him at another. They give themselves only to be caressed, and wrest themselves back again, when they are crucified; or at least turn for consolation to the creature.

2. No, beloved souls, you will not find consolation in aught but in the love of the cross, and in total abandonment; who savoreth not the cross, savoreth not the things that be of God. (See Matt. xvi. 23.) It is impossible to love God without loving the cross; and a heart that savors the cross, finds the bitterest things to be sweet; *"To the hungry soul every bitter thing is sweet;"* (Prov. xxvii. 7:) because it finds itself hungering for God, in proportion as it is hungering for the cross. God gives us the cross, and the cross gives us God.

We may be assured that there is an internal advancement, when there is progress in the way of the cross; abandonment and the cross go hand in hand together.

3. As soon as anything is presented in the form of suffering, and you feel a repugnance, resign yourself immediately to God with respect to it, and give yourself up to Him in sacrifice: you will then find, that when the cross arrives, it will not be so very burthensome, because you have yourself desired it. This, however does not prevent you from feeling its weight, as some have imagined; for when we do not feel the cross, we do not suffer. A

sensibility to suffering is one of the principal parts of suffering itself. Jesus Christ himself chose to endure its utmost rigors. We often bear the cross in weakness, at other times in strength; all should be alike to us in the will of God.

CHAPTER VIII.

1. On mysteries; God gives them in this state in reality.

2, 3. We must let Him bestow or withhold as seems good to Him, with a loving regard to his will.

It will be objected, that, by this method, we shall have no mysteries imprinted on our minds; but so far is this from bring the case, that it is the peculiar means of imparting them to the soul. Jesus Christ, to whom we are abandoned, and whom we follow as the way, whom we hear as the truth, and who animates us as the life (John xiv. 6,) in imprinting himself on the soul, impresses there the characters of his different states. To bear all the states of Jesus Christ, is a much greater thing, than merely to meditate about them. St. Paul bore in his body the states of Jesus Christ; *"I bear in my body, "* says he, *"the marks of the Lord Jesus;"* (Gal. vi. 17;) he does not say that he reasoned thereon.

2. In this state of abandonment Jesus Christ frequently communicates some peculiar views, or revelations of his states: these we should thankfully accept, and dispose ourselves for what appears to be his will; receiving equally whatever frame He may bestow, and having no other choice, but that of ardently reaching after Him, of dwelling ever with Him, and of sinking into nothingness before Him, and accepting indiscriminately all his gifts, whether darkness or illumination, fecundity or barrenness, weakness or strength, sweetness or bitterness, temptations, distractions, pain, weariness, or uncertainty; and none of all these should, for one moment, retard our course.

3. God engages some, for whole years, in the contemplation and enjoyment of a single mystery, the simple view or contemplation of which recollects the soul; let them be faithful to it; but as soon as God is pleased to withdraw this view from the soul, let it freely yield to the deprivation. Some are very uneasy at their inability to meditate on certain mysteries; but without reason, since an affectionate attachment to God includes in itself every species of devotion, and whoever is calmly united to God alone, is, indeed, most excellently and effectually applied to every divine mystery.

Whoever loves God loves all that appertains to him.

CHAPTER IX.

1.2. On virtue. All virtues come with God and are solidly and deeply implanted in the soul in this degree of the prayer of the heart.

3. This takes place without difficulty.

It is thus that we acquire virtue with facility and certainty; for as God is the principle of all virtues, we inherit all in the possession of Himself; and in proportion as we approach toward his possession, in like proportion do we receive the most eminent virtues. For all virtue is but as a mask, an outside appearance mutable as our garments, if it be not bestowed from within; then, indeed, it is genuine, essential, and permanent: *"The King's daughter is all glorious within,"* says David. (Psalm xlv. 13.) These souls, above all others, practice virtue in the most eminent degree, though they advert not to any particular virtue. God, to whom they are united, leads them to the most extensive practice of it; He is exceedingly jealous over them, and permits them not the least pleasure.

2. What a hungering for sufferings have those souls, who thus glow with divine love! How would

they precipitate themselves into excessive austerities, where they permitted to pursue their own inclinations! They think of nought save how they may please their Beloved; and they begin to neglect and forget themselves; and as their love to God increases, so do self-detestation and disregard of the creature.

3. O were this simple method once acquired, a way so suited to all, to the dull and ignorant as well as to the most learned, how easily would the whole church of God be reformed! Love only is required: *"Love,"* says St. Augustine, *"and then do what you please."* For when we truly love, we cannot have so much as a will to do anything that might offend the object of our affections.

CHAPTER X.

1. On mortification: that it is never perfect when it is solely exterior.

2. But it must be accomplished by dwelling upon God within.

3. Which, however, does not dispense with its outward practice to some degree.

4. Hence, a sound conversion.

I say further, that, in any other way, it is next to impossible to acquire a perfect mortification of the senses and passions.

The reason is obvious: the soul gives vigor and energy to the senses, and the senses raise and stimulate the passions; a dead body has neither sensations nor passions, because its connection with the soul is dissolved. All endeavors merely to rectify the exterior impel the soul yet farther outward into that about which it is so warmly and zealously engaged. Its powers are diffused and scattered abroad; for, its whole attention being immediately directed to austerities and other externals, it thus invigorates those very senses it is aiming to subdue. For the senses have no other spring whence to derive their vigor than the application of the soul to themselves, the degree of their live and activity being proportioned to the degree of attention which the soul bestows upon them. This life of the senses stirs up and provokes the passions, instead of suppressing or subduing them; austerities may indeed enfeeble the body, but for the reasons just mentioned, can never take off the keenness of the senses, nor lessen their activity.

2. The only method of effecting this, is inward recollection, by which the soul is turned wholly

and altogether inward, to possess a present God. If it direct all its vigor and energy within, this simple act separates it from the senses, and, employing all its powers internally, it renders them faint; and the nearer it draws to God, the farther is it separated from self. Hence it is, that those in whom the attractions of grace are very powerful, find the outward man altogether weak and feeble, and even liable to faintings.

3. I do not mean by this, to discourage mortification; for it should ever accompany prayer, according to the strength and state of the person, or as obedience demands. But I say, that mortification should not be our principal exercise; nor should we prescribe to ourselves such and such austerities, but simply following the internal attractions of grace, and being occupied with the divine presence, without thinking particularly on mortification, God will enable us to perform every species of it. He gives those who abide faithful to their abandonment to Him, no relaxation until He has subdued everything in them that remains to be mortified.

We have only, then, to continue steadfast in the utmost attention to God, and all things will be perfectly done. All are not capable of outward austerities, but all are capable of this. In the mortification of the eye and ear, which continually supply the busy imagination with new subjects, there is little danger of falling into excess; but God will teach us this also, and we have only to follow his Spirit.

4. The soul has a double advantage by proceeding thus; for, in withdrawing from outward objects, it constantly draws nearer to God; and besides the secret sustaining and preserving power and virtue which it receives, it is farther removed from sin the nearer it comes to Him; so that its conversion becomes firmly established as a matter of habit.

CHAPTER XI.

1. On the perfect conversion which is the result of this kind of prayer; how it is accomplished.

2, 3. Two of its aids; the drawing of God, and the tendency of the soul to its centre.

4. Its practice.

"Turn ye unto Him from whom the children of Israel have so deeply revolted." (Isa. xxxi. 6.) Conversion is nothing more than turning from the creature in order to return to God.

It is not perfect (however good and essential to salvation) when it consists simply in turning from sin to grace. To be complete, it should take place from without inwardly.

When the soul is once turned toward God, it finds a wonderful facility in continuing steadfast in conversion; and the longer it remains thus converted, the nearer it approaches and the more firmly it adheres to God; and the nearer it draws to Him, it is of necessity the farther removed from the creature, which is so contrary to Him; so that it is so effectually established in conversion, that the state becomes habitual, and as it were natural.

Now, we must not suppose that this is effected by a violent exertion of its own powers; for it is not capable of, nor should it attempt any other co-operation with divine grace, than that of endeavoring to withdraw itself from external objects, and to turn inwards; after which it has nothing farther to do, than to continue firm in its adherence to God.

2. God has an *attractive virtue* which draws the soul more and more powerfully to Himself, and in attracting, He purifies; just as it is with a gross vapor exhaled by the sun, which, as it gradually ascends, is rarified and rendered pure; the vapor, indeed, contributes to its ascent only by its

passivity; but the soul co-operates freely and voluntarily.

This kind of introversion is very easy and advances the soul naturally, and without effort, because God is our centre. The centre always exerts a very powerful attractive virtue; and the more spiritual and exalted it is, the more violent and irresistible are its attractions.

3. But besides the attracting virtue of the centre, there is, in every creature, *a strong tendency to reunion* with its centre, which is vigorous and active in proportion to the spirituality and perfection of the subject.

As soon as anything is turned towards its centre, it is precipitated towards it with extreme rapidity, unless it be withheld by some invincible obstacle. A stone held in the hand is no sooner disengaged than by its own weight it falls to the earth as to its centre; so also water and fire, when unobstructed, flow incessantly towards their centre. Now, when the soul by its efforts to recollect itself, is brought into the influence of the central tendency, it falls gradually, without any other force than the weight of love, into its proper centre; and the more passive and tranquil it remains, the the freer from self-motion, the more rapidly it advances, because the energy of the central attractive virtue is unobstructed, and has full liberty for action.[6]

4. All our care should therefore be directed towards acquiring the greatest degree of inward recollection; nor should we be discouraged by the difficulties we encounter in this exercise, which will soon be recompensed on the part of God, by such abundant supplies of grace, as will render it perfectly easy, provided we are faithful in meekly

---

[6] This beautiful image comprehends the whole essence of the divine life, as understood by the teachers of the interior, and seems to contain as much truth as beauty. God is the great magnet of the soul, but of that only; and impurity or admixture prevents his full attractive power. If there were nothing of the kind in the soul, it would rush, under this all-powerful attraction, with irresistible and instantaneous speed, to be lost in God. But many load themselves with goods, or seize some part of earth or self with so tenacious a grasp, that they spend their whole lives without advancing at more than a snail's pace towards their centre; and it is only when God in love strikes their burden violently from their hands, that they begin to be conscious of the hinderance that detained them. If we will only suffer every weight to drop, and withdraw our hands from self, and every creature, there will be but little interval between our sacrifice and our resurrection. Some pious persons have objected to the passivity here inculcated, as though the soul were required to become dead, like an inanimate object, in order that God might do his pleasure with it. But this objection will vanish if it be considered that the life of the soul is in the will, and that this condition of utter passivity implies the highest state of activity of the will, in willing without any cessation, and with all its powers, that the will of God shall be done in it, and by it, and through it. See this further insisted upon in chapter xxi.-Editor.

withdrawing our hearts from outward distractions and occupations, and returning to our centre, with *affections* full of tenderness and serenity. When at any time the passions are turbulent, a gentle retreat inwards to a present God, easily deadens them; any other way of opposing rather irritates than appeases them.

CHAPTER XII.

1. Another and more exalted degree of prayer, the prayer of the simple presence of God, or of Active Contemplation, of which very little is said, the subject being reserved for another treatise.

2, 3, 4. How selfish activity merges here in an activity lively, full, abundant, divine, easy, and as it were natural; a state far different from that idleness and passivity objected to by the opponents of the inner life. The subject illustrated by several comparisons.

5. Transition to Infused Prayer, in which the fundamental, vital activity of the soul is not lost, but is more abundantly and powerfully influenced (as are the faculties) by that of God.

6. The facility of these methods of coming to God, and an exhortation to self abandonment.

The soul that is faithful in the exercise of love and adherence to God, as above described, is astonished to feel Him gradually taking possession of its whole being; it now enjoys a continual sense of that presence which is become as it were natural to it; and this, as well as prayer, becomes a matter of habit. It feels an unusual serenity gradually diffusing itself over all its faculties. Silence now constitutes its whole prayer; whilst God communicates an infused love, which is the beginning of ineffable blessedness.

O that I were permitted to pursue this subject, and describe some degrees of the endless progression of subsequent states? But I now write only for beginners; and shall therefore proceed no farther, but wait our Lord's time for developing what may be applicable to every state.[7]

2. We must, however, urge it as a matter of the highest import, to cease self-action and self-exertion, that God himself may act alone: He says by the mouth of his prophet David, *"Be still and know that I am God."* (Psalm xlvi. 10.) But the centre is so infatuated with love and attachment to

_____

[7] A design subsequently carried out in the work entitled "The Torrents," and less diffusely in the "Concise View," follows the present treatise.-Editor.

its own working, that it does not believe that it works at all unless it can feel, know, and distinguish all its operations. It is ignorant that its inability minutely to observe the manner of its motion, is occasioned by the swiftness of its progress; and that the operations of God, abounding more and more, absorb those of the creature; just as we see that the stars shine brightly before the sun rises, but gradually vanish as his light advances, and become invisible, not from want of light in themselves, but from the excess of it in him.

The case is similar here; for there is a strong and universal light which absorbs all the little distinct lights of the soul; they grow faint and disappear under its powerful influence, and self-activity is now no longer distinguishable.

3. Those greatly err, who accuse this prayer of inactivity, a charge that can only arise from inexperience. O! if they would but make some efforts towards the attainment of it, they would soon become full of light and knowledge in relation to it.

This appearance of inaction is, indeed, not the consequence of sterility, but of abundance, as will be clearly perceived by the experienced soul, who will recognize that the silence is full and unctuous by reason of plenty.

4. There are two kinds of people that keep silence; the one because they have nothing to say, the other because they have too much: the latter is the case in this state; silence is occasioned by excess and not by defect.

To be drowned, and to die of thirst, are deaths widely different; yet water may be said to be the cause of both; abundance destroys in one case, and want in the other. So here the fullness of grace stills the activity of self; and therefore it is of the utmost importance to remain as silent as possible.

The infant hanging at its mother's breast, is a lively illustration of our subject; it begins to draw the milk, by moving its little lips; but when its nourishment flows abundantly, it is content to swallow without effort; by any other course it would only hurt itself, spill the milk, and be obliged to quit the breast.

We must act in like manner in the beginning of prayer, by moving the lips of the affections; but as soon as the milk of divine grace flows freely, we have nothing to do, but, in stillness, sweetly to imbibe it, and when it ceases to flow, again stir up the affections as the infant moves its lips. Whoever acts otherwise, cannot make the best use of this grace, which is bestowed to allure the soul *into the repose of* Love, and not to force it into the multiplicity of self.

5. But what becomes of the babe that thus gently and without exertion, drinks in the milk? Who would believe that it could thus receive nourishment? Yet the more peacefully it feeds, the better it thrives. What, I say, becomes of this infant? It drops asleep on its mother's bosom. So the soul that is tranquil and peaceful in prayer, sinks frequently into a mystic slumber, wherein all its powers are at rest, till it is wholly fitted for that state, of which it enjoys these transient anticipations. You see that in this process the soul is led naturally, without trouble, effort, art or study.

The interior is not a strong hold, to be taken by storm and violence; but a kingdom of peace, which is to be gained only by love. If any will thus pursue the little path I have pointed out, it will lead them to *infused prayer.* God demands nothing extraordinary nor too difficult; on the contrary, He is greatly pleased by a simple and child-like conduct.

6. The most sublime attainments in religion, are those which are easiest reached; the most necessary ordinances are the least difficult. It is thus also in natural things; if you would reach the sea, embark on a river, and you will be conveyed to it insensibly and without exertion. Would you go to God, follow this sweet and simple path, and you will arrive at the desired object, with an ease and expedition that will amaze you.

O that you would but once make the trial! how soon would you find that all I have said is too little, and that your own experience will carry you infinitely beyond it! What is it you fear? why do you not instantly cast yourself into the arms of Love, who only extended them on the cross that He might embrace you? What risk do you run in depending solely on God, and abandoning yourself wholly to Him? Ah! he will not deceive you, unless by bestowing an abundance beyond your highest hopes; but those who expect all from themselves, may hear this rebuke of God by his prophet Isaiah, *"Ye have wearied yourselves in the multiplicity of your ways, and have not said, let us rest in peace."* (Isa. lvii. 10, vulgate.)

MADAME GUYON

CHAPTER XIII.

1. On the rest before God present in the soul in a wonderful way.

2. Fruits of this peaceful presence.

3. Practical advice.

The soul advanced thus far, has no need of any other preparation than its quietude: for now the presence of God, during the day, which is the great effect, or rather continuation of prayer, begins to be *infused, and almost without intermission.* The soul certainly enjoys transcendent blessedness, and finds that God is more intimately present to it than it is to itself.

The only way to find him is by introversion. No sooner do the bodily eyes close, than the soul is wrapt in prayer: it is amazed at so great a blessing, and enjoys an internal converse, which external matters cannot interrupt.

2. The same may be said of this species of prayer, that is said of wisdom: *"all good things come together with her."* (Wisdom vii. 11.) For virtues flow from this soul into exercise with so much sweetness and facility, that they appear natural to it, and the living spring within breaks forth

abundantly into a facility for all goodness, and an insensibility to all evil.

3. Let it then remain faithful in this state; and beware of choosing or seeking any other disposition whatever than this simple rest, as a preparative either to confession or communion, to action or prayer; for its sole business is to suffer itself to be filled with this divine effusion. I would not be understood to speak of the preparations necessary for ordinances, but of the most interior disposition in which they can be received.

CHAPTER XIV.

1, 2. On interior silence; its reason; God recommends it.

3. Exterior silence, retirement and recollection contribute to it.

"The Lord is in his holy temple; let all the earth keep silence before him." (Hab. ii. 20.) The reason why inward silence is so indispensable, is, because the Word is essential and eternal, and necessarily requires dispositions in the soul in some degree correspondent to His nature, as a capacity for the reception of Himself. Hearing is a sense formed to receive sounds, and is rather passive than active, admitting, but not communicating sensation; and

if we would hear, we must lend the ear for that purpose. Christ, the eternal Word, who must be communicated to the soul to give it new life, requires the most intense attention to his voice, when He would speak within us.

2. Hence it is so frequently enjoined upon us in sacred writ, to listen and be attentive to the voice of God; I quote a few of the numerous exhortations to this effect: *"Hearken unto me, my people, and give ear unto me, O my nation!"* (Isa. li. 4,) and again *"Hear me, all ye whom I carry in my bosom, and bear within my bowels:"* (Isa. xlvi. 3,) and further by the Psalmist, *"Hearken, O daughter! and consider, and incline thine ear; forget also thine own people, and thy father's house; so shall the king greatly desire thy beauty."* (Ps. xlv. 10, 11.)

We must *forget ourselves,* and all self-interest, and listen and be attentive to God; these two simple actions, or rather passive dispositions, produce the love of that beauty, which He himself communicates.

3. Outward silence is very requisite for the cultivation and improvement of inward; and, indeed, it is impossible we should become truly interior, without loving silence and retirement.

God saith by the mouth of his prophet, *"I will lead her into solitude, and there will I speak to her heart* (Hos. ii. 14, vulg.); and unquestionably the being internally engaged with God is wholly incompatible with being externally busied about a thousand trifles.

When, through weakness, we become as it were uncentered, we must immediately turn again inward; and this process we must repeat as often as our distractions recur. It is a small matter to be devout and recollected for an hour or half hour, if the unction and spirit of prayer do not continue with us during the whole day.

CHAPTER XV.

1, 2. On the examination of conscience; how it is performed in this state, and that by God himself.

3, 4. On the confession, contrition, and forgetfulness or remembrance of faults in this state.

5. This is not applicable to the previous degree, Communion.

Self-examination should always precede confession, but the manner of it should be conformable to the state of the soul. The business of those that are advanced to the degree of which we now treat, is to lay their whole souls open before God, who will not fail to enlighten them, and enable them to see the peculiar nature of their faults. This examination, however, should be peaceful and tranquil; and we should depend on God for the discovery and knowledge of our sins, rather than on the diligence of our own scrutiny.

When we examine with effort, we are easily deceived, and betrayed by self-love into error: *"We call the evil good, and the good evil,"* (Isa. v. 20); but when we lie in full exposure before the Sun of Righteousness, his divine beams render the smallest atoms visible. We must, then, forsake self, and abandon our souls to God, as well in examination as confession.

2. When souls have attained to this species of prayer, no fault escapes the reprehension of God; no sooner are they committed than they are rebuked by an inward burning and tender confusion. Such is the scrutiny of Him who suffers no evil to be concealed; and the only way is to turn simply to God, and bear the pain and correction He inflicts.

As He becomes the incessant examiner of the soul, it can now no longer examine itself; and if it be faithful in its abandonment, experience will prove that it is much more effectually explored by his divine light, than by all its own carefulness.

3. Those who tread these paths should be informed of a matter respecting their confusion, in which they are apt to err. When they begin to give an account of their sins, instead of the regret and contrition they had been accustomed to feel, they find that love and tranquility sweetly pervade and take possession of their souls: now those who are not properly instructed are desirous of resisting this sensation, and forming an act of contrition, because they have heard, and with truth, that this is requisite. But they are not aware that they thereby lose the genuine contrition, which is *this infused love,* and which infinitely surpasses any effect produced by self-exertion, comprehending the other acts in itself as in one principal act, in much higher perfection than if they were distinctly perceived.

Let them not be troubled to do otherwise, when God acts so excellently in and for them. To hate sin in this manner, is to hate it as God does. The purest love is that which is of his immediate operation in the soul; why should we then be so eager for action? Let us remain in the state He assigns us, agreeably to the instructions of the wise man: *"Put your confidence in God; remain in quiet where he hath placed you."* (Eccles. xi. 22.)

4. The soul will also be amazed at finding a difficulty in calling its faults to remembrance. This, however, should cause no uneasiness, first, because this forgetfulness of our faults is some proof of our purification from them, and, in this degree of advancement, it is best to forget whatever concerns ourselves that we may remember only God. Secondly, because, when confession is our duty, God will not fail to make known to us our greatest faults; for then He himself examines; and the soul will feel the end of examination more perfectly accomplished, than it could possibly have been by all our own endeavors.

5. These instructions, however, would be altogether unsuitable to the preceding degrees, while the soul continues in its active state, wherein it is right and necessary that it should an all things exert itself, in proportion to its advancement. As to those who have arrived at this more advanced state, I exhort them to follow these instructions, and not to vary their simple occupations even on approaching the communion; let them remain in silence, and suffer God to act freely. He cannot be better received than by Himself.

A SHORT AND VERY EASY METHOD OF PRAYER

CHAPTER XVI.

1. On reading and vocal prayers; they should be limited.

2. Not to be used against our interior drawing, unless they are of obligation.

The method of reading in this state, is to cease when you feel yourself recollected, and remain in stillness, reading but little, and always desisting when thus internally attracted.

2. The soul that is called to a state of inward silence, should not encumber itself with vocal prayers; whenever it makes use of them, and finds a difficulty therein, and an attraction to silence, let it not use constraint by persevering, but yield to the internal drawing, unless the repeating such prayers be a matter of obligation. In any other case, it is much better not to set forms, but wholly given up to the leadings of the Holy Spirit; and in this way every species of devotion is fulfilled in a most eminent degree.

CHAPTER XVII.

1. On petitions; those which are self-originated cease; and their place is supplied by those of the Spirit of God.

2. Abandonment and faith necessary here.

The soul should not be surprised at feeling itself unable to offer up to God such petitions as had formerly been made with facility; for now the Spirit maketh intercession for it according to the will of God; that Spirit which helpeth our infirmities; *"for we know not what we should pray for as we ought; but the Spirit itself maketh intercession for us with groanings which cannot be uttered."* (Rom. viii. 26.) We must second the designs of God, which tend to divest us of all our own operations, that his may be substituted in their place.

2. Let this, then, be done in you; and suffer not yourself to be attached to anything, however good it may appear; it is no longer such to you, if it in any measure turns you aside from what God desires of you. For the divine will is preferable to every other good. Shake off, then, all self-interest, and live by faith and abandonment; here it is that genuine *faith* begins truly to operate.

CHAPTER XVIII.

1. On faults committed in the state. We must turn from them to God without trouble or discouragement.

2. The contrary course weakens us and is opposed to the practice of humble souls.

Should we either wander among externals, or commit a fault, we must instantly turn inwards; for having departed thereby from God, we should as soon as possible turn toward Him, and suffer the penalty which He inflicts.

It is of great importance to guard against vexation on account of our faults; it springs from a secret root of pride, and a love of our own excellence; we are hurt at feeling what we are.

2. If we become discouraged, we are the more enfeebled; and from our reflections on our imperfections, a chagrin arises, which is often worse than the imperfection themselves.

The truly humble soul is not surprised at its defects or failings; and the more miserable it beholds itself, the more it abandons itself to God, and presses for a more intimate alliance with Him, seeing the need it has of his aid. We should the rather be induced to act thus, as God himself has said, *"I will instruct thee and teach thee in the way which thou shalt go; I will guide thee with mine eye."* (Psalm xxxii. 8.)

CHAPTER XIX.

1. On distractions and temptations; the remedy for them is to turn to God.

2. This is the practice of the saints, and there is danger in any other way.

A direct struggle with distractions and temptations rather serves to augment them, and withdraws the soul from that adherence to God, which should ever be its sole occupation. We should simply turn away from the evil, and draw yet nearer to God. A little child, on perceiving a monster, does not wait to fight with it, and will scarcely turn its eyes toward it, but quickly shrinks into the bosom of its mother, in assurance of its safety. *"God is in the midst of her,"* says the Psalmist, *"she shall not be moved; God shall help her, and that right early."* (Psalm xlvi. 5.)

2. If we do otherwise, and in our weakness attempt to attack our enemies, we shall frequently find ourselves wounded, if not totally defeated: but, by remaining in the simple presence of God, we shall find instant supplies of strength for our support. This was the resource of David: *"I have set,"* says he, *"the Lord always before me; because he is at my right hand, I shall not be moved. Therefore my*

heart is glad, and my glory rejoiceth; my flesh also shall rest in hope." (Psalm xvi. 8, 9.) And it is said in Exodus, *"The Lord shall fight for you, and ye shall hold your peace."* (Exod. xiv. 14.)

CHAPTER XX.

1, 2. Prayer divinely explained as a devotional sacrifice, under the similitude of incense.

3. Our annihilation in this sacrifice.

4, 5. Solidity and fruit of this prayer according to the Gospel.

Both devotion and sacrifice are comprehended in prayer, which, according to St. John is an incense, the smoke whereof ascendeth unto God; therefore it is said in the Apocalypse, that *"unto the angel was given much incense, that he should offer it with the prayers of all saints."* (Rev. viii. 3.)

Prayer is the effusion of the heart in the presence of God: *"I have poured out my soul before the Lord,"* said the mother of Samuel. (1 Sam. i. 15.) The prayer of the wise men at the feet of Christ in the stable of Bethlehem, was signified by the incense they offered.

2. Prayer is a certain warmth of love, melting, dissolving, and sublimating the soul, and causing

it to ascend unto God, and, as the soul is melted, odors rise from it; and these sweet exhalations proceed from the consuming fire of love within.

This is illustrated in the *Canticles,* (i. 12,) where the spouse says, *"While the king sitteth at his table, my spikenard sendeth forth the smell thereof."* The table is the centre of the soul; and when God is there, and we know how to dwell near, and abide with Him, the sacred presence gradually dissolves the hardness of the soul, and, as it melts, fragrance issues forth; hence it is, that the Beloved says of his spouse, in seeing her soul melt when he spoke, *"Who is this that cometh out of the wilderness, like pillars of smoke perfumed with myrrh and frankincense?"* (Cant. v. 6; iii. 6.)

3. Thus does the soul ascend to God, by giving up self to the destroying and annihilating power of divine love. This is a state of sacrifice essential to the Christian religion, in which the soul suffers itself to be destroyed and annihilated, that it may pay homage to the sovereignty of God; as it is written, *"The power of the Lord is great, and he is honored only by the humble."* (Eccles. iii. 20.) By the destruction of self, we acknowledge the supreme existence of God. We must cease to exist in self, in order that the Spirit of the Eternal Word may exist in us: it is by the giving up of our own

life, that we give place to his coming; and in dying to ourselves, He himself lives in us.

We must surrender our whole being to Christ Jesus, and cease to live any longer in ourselves, that He may become our life; *that being dead, our life may be hid with Christ in God."* (Col. iii. 3.) *"Pass ye into me,"* sayeth God, *"all ye who earnestly seek after me."* (Eccles. xxi. 16.) But how is it we pass into God? In no way but by leaving and forsaking ourselves, that we may be lost in Him; and this can be effected only by annihilation, which, being the true prayer of adoration, renders unto God alone, all *blessing, honor, glory, and power, forever and ever."* (Rev. v. 13.)

4. This prayer of truth; it is *"worshipping God in spirit and in truth:"* (John iv. 23.) *"In spirit,"* because we enter into the purity of that Spirit which prayeth within us, and are drawn forth from our own carnal and human method; *"in truth,"* because we are thereby placed in the truth of the all of God, and the nothing of the creature.

There are but these two truths, the All and the Nothing; everything else is falsehood. We can pay due honor to the All of God, only in our own Annihilation; which is no sooner accomplished, that He, who never suffers a void in nature, instantly fills us with Himself.

Ah! did we but know the virtues and the blessings which the soul derives from this prayer, we should not be willing to do anything else; It is the *pearl of great price; the hidden treasure,* (Matt. xiii. 44, 45,) which, whoever findeth, selleth freely all that he hath to purchase it; it is the *well of living water, which springeth up unto everlasting life.* It is the adoration of God *"in spirit and in truth:"* (John iv. 14–23:) and it is the full performance of the purest evangelical precepts.

5. Jesus Christ assures us, that the *"kingdom of God is within us:"* (Luke xvii. 21:) and this is true in two senses: first, when God becomes so fully Saviour and Lord in us, that nothing resists his domination, then our interior is his kingdom; and again, when we possess God, who is the Supreme Good, we possess his kingdom also, wherein there is fulness of joy, and where we attain the end of our creation. Thus it is said, *"to serve God is to reign."* The end of our creation, indeed, is to enjoy God, even in this life; but, alas! who thinks of it?

CHAPTER XXI.

The objections of slothfulness and inactivity made to this form of prayer fully met, and the truth shown that the soul acts nobly, forcibly, calmly, quickly, freely, simply, sweetly, temperately, and certainly; but in dependence upon God, and moved by his Holy Spirit: the restless and selfish activity of nature being destroyed, and the life of God communicated by union with Him.

Some persons, when they hear of the prayer of silence, falsely imagine *that the soul remains stupid, dead, and inactive;* but it unquestionably acts more nobly and more extensively than it had ever done before; for God himself is its mover, and it now acts by the agency of his Spirit. St. Paul would have us *led by the Spirit of God.* (Rom. viii. 14.)

It is not meant that we should cease from action; but that we should act through the internal agency of his grace. This is finely represented by the prophet Ezekiel's vision of the wheels, which had a living Spirit; and whithersoever the Spirit was to go, they went; they ascended and descended as they were moved; for the Spirit of life was in them, and they returned not when they went. (Ezek. i. 18.) Thus the soul should be equally subservient to the will of that vivifying Spirit which is in it, and scrupulously faithful to follow only as that moves. These motions never tend to return in reflections on the creatures or self; but go forward in an incessant approach toward the end.

2. This *activity* of the soul is attended with the utmost tranquility. When it acts of itself, the act is forced and constrained, and, therefore, it is more easily distinguished; but when the action is under the influence of the Spirit of grace, it is so free, so easy, and so natural, that it almost seems as if we did not act at all. *"He brought me forth also into a large place; He delivered me, because He delighted in me."* (Ps. xviii. 19.)

When the soul is in its central tendency, or in other words, is returned through recollection into itself, from that moment, the central attraction becomes a most potent activity, infinitely surpassing in energy every other species. Nothing, indeed, can equal the swiftness of this tendency to the centre; and though an activity, yet it is so noble, so peaceful, so full of tranquility, so natural, and so spontaneous, that it appears to the soul as if it were none at all.

When a wheel rolls slowly we can easily perceive its parts; but when its motion is rapid, we can

A SHORT AND VERY EASY METHOD OF PRAYER

distinguish nothing. So the soul which rests in God, has an activity exceedingly noble and elevated, yet altogether peaceful; and the more peaceful it is, the swifter is its course; because it is given up to that Spirit by whom it is moved and directed.

3. This attracting Spirit is no other than God himself, who, in drawing us, causes us to run to Him. How well did the spouse understand this, when she said, *"Draw me, we will run after thee."* (Cant. i. 4.) Draw me unto Thee, O my divine centre, by the secret springs of my existence, and all my powers and senses shall follow Thee! This simple attraction is both an ointment to heal and a perfume to allure: *we follow,* saith she, *the fragrance of thy perfumes;* and though so *powerful* an attraction, it is followed by the soul *freely*, and without constraint; for it is equally delighted as forcible; and whilst it attracts by its power, it carries us away by its sweetness. *"Draw me,"* says the spouse, *"and we will run after thee."* She speaks of and to herself: "*draw me,*"—behold the unity of the centre which is drawn! *"we will run,"*—behold the correspondence and course of all the senses and powers in following the attraction of the centre!

4. Instead, then, of encouraging sloth, we promote the highest activity, by inculcating a *total dependence of the Spirit of God,* as our moving principle; for it *is in Him, and by Him alone, that we live and move, and have our being.* (Acts xvii. 28.) This meek dependence on the Spirit of God is indispensably necessary, and causes the soul shortly to attain the unity and simplicity in which it was created.

We must, therefore, forsake our multifarious activity, to enter into the simplicity and unity of God, in whose image we were originally formed. (Gen. i. 27.) *"The Spirit is one and manifold,* (Wisdom vii. 22,) and his unity does not preclude his multiplicity. We enter into his unity when we are united to his Spirit, and by that means have one and the same spirit with Him; and we are multiplied in respect to the outward execution of his will, without any departure from our state of union.

In this way, when we are wholly moved by the divine Spirit, which is infinitely active, our activity must, indeed, be more energetic than that which is merely our own. We must yield ourselves to the guidance of *"wisdom, which is more moving than any motion,"* (Wisdom vii. 24,) and by abiding in dependence upon its action, our activity will be truly efficient.

5. *"All things were made by the Word, and without Him was not anything made, that was made."* (John i. 3.) God originally formed us *in his own image and likeness;* He breathed into us the Spirit of his Word, that breath of Life (Gen. ii. 7) which He gave us at our creation, in the participation whereof the image of God consisted. Now, this Life is one, simple, pure, intimate, and always fruitful.

The devil having broken and deformed the divine image in the soul by sin, the agency of the same Word whose Spirit was inbreathed at our creation, is absolutely necessary for its renovation. It was necessary that it should be He, because He is the express image of his Father; and no image can be repaired by its own efforts, but must remain passive for that purpose under the hand of the workman.

Our *activity* should, therefore, consist in placing ourselves in a state of susceptibility to divine impressions, and pliability to all the operations of the Eternal Word. Whilst tablet is unsteady, the painter is unable to produce a correct picture upon it, and every movement of self is productive of erroneous lineaments; it interrupts the work and defeats the design of this adorable Painter. We must then remain in peace, and move only when He moves us. *Jesus Christ hath life in himself,* (John v. 26,) and He must give life to every living thing.

The spirit of the church of God is the spirit of the divine movement. Is she idle, barren, or unfruitful? No; she acts, but her activity is in dependence upon the Spirit of God, who moves and governs her. Just so should it be in her members; that they may be spiritual children of the Church, they must be moved by the Spirit.

6. As all action is estimable only in proportion to the grandeur and dignity of the efficient principle, this action is incontestably more noble than any other. Actions produced by a divine principle, are *divine;* but creaturely actions, however good they appear, are only *human,* or at least virtuous, even when accompanied by grace.

Jesus Christ says that He has life in Himself: all other beings have only a borrowed life; but the Word has life in Himself; and being communicative of his nature, He desires to bestow it upon man. We should therefore make room for the influx of this life, which can only be done by the ejection and loss of the Adamical life, and the suppression of the activity of self. This is agreeable to the assertion of St. Paul, *"If any man be in Christ, he is a new creature; old things are passed away; behold, all things are become new,"* (2 Cor. v. 17;) but this state can be accomplished only by dying to ourselves, and to all our own activity, that the activity of God may be substituted in its place.

Instead, therefore, of prohibiting activity, we enjoin it; but in absolute dependence on the Spirit of God, that his activity may take the place of our own. This can only be effected by the consent of the creature; and this concurrence can only be yielded by moderating our own action, that the activity of God may, little by little, be wholly substituted for it.

7. Jesus Christ has exemplified this in the Gospel. Martha did what was right; but because she did it in her own spirit, Christ rebuked her. The spirit of man is restless and turbulent; for which reason he does little, though he seems to do a great deal. *"Martha,"* says Christ, *"thou art careful and troubled about many things; but one thing is needful; and Mary hath chosen that good part which shall not be taken away from her."* (Luke x. 41, 42.) And what was it Mary had chosen? Repose, tranquility, and peace. She had apparently

ceased to act, that the Spirit of Christ might act in her; she had ceased to live, that Christ might be her life.

This shows how necessary it is to renounce ourselves, and all our activity, to follow Christ; for we cannot follow Him, if we are not animated by his Spirit. Now that his Spirit may gain admittance, it is necessary that our own should be expelled: *"He that is joined unto the Lord,"* says St. Paul, *"is one spirit."* (1 Cor. vi. 17.) And David said it was good for him to draw near unto the Lord, and to put his trust in him. (Psalm lxxiii. 28.) What is this drawing near? it is the beginning of union.

8. Divine union has its commencement, its progress, its achievement, and its consummation. It is at first an inclination towards God. When the soul is introverted in the manner before described, it gets within the influence of the central attraction, and acquires an eager desire after union; this is the beginning. It then adheres to Him when it has got nearer and nearer, and finally becomes one, that is, one spirit with Him; and then it is that spirit which had wandered from God, returns again to its end.

9. Into this way, then, which is the divine motion, and the spirit of Jesus Christ, we must necessarily enter. St. Paul says, *"If any man have not the spirit of Christ, he is none of his"* (Rom. viii. 9): therefore, to be Christ's, we must be filled with his Spirit, and emptied of our own. The Apostle, in the same passage, proved the necessity of this divine influence. *"As many,"* says he, *"as are led by the Spirit of God, they are the sons of God."* (Rom. viii. 14.)

The spirit of divine filiation is, then, the spirit of divine motion: he therefore adds, *"Ye have not received the spirit of bondage again to fear; but ye have received the spirit of adoption whereby ye cry Abba, Father."* This spirit is no other than the spirit of Christ, through which we participate in his filiation; *"The Spirit beareth witness with our spirit that we are the children of God."*

When the soul yields itself to the influence of this blessed Spirit, it perceives the testimony of its divine filiation; and it feels also, with superadded joy, that *it has received, not the spirit of bondage, but of liberty, even the liberty of the children of God;* it then finds that it acts freely and sweetly, though with vigor and infallibility.

10. The spirit of divine action is so necessary in all things, that St. Paul, in the same passage, founds that necessity on our ignorance with respect to what we pray for: *"The Spirit,"* says he, *"also helpeth our infirmities: for we know not what we should pray for as we ought; but the Spirit itself maketh intercession for us, with groanings which cannot be uttered."* This is plain enough; if we know not what we stand in need of, nor how to pray as we ought for those things which are necessary, and if the Spirit which is in us, and to which we resign ourselves, must ask for us, should we not permit Him to give vent to his unutterable groanings in our behalf?

This Spirit is the Spirit of the Word, which is always heard, as He says himself: *"I knew that thou hearest me always;"* (John xi. 42;) and if we freely admit this Spirit to pray and intercede for us, we also shall be always heard. And why? Let us learn from the same great Apostle, that skillful Mystic, and Master of the interior life, where he adds, *"He that searcheth the heart, knoweth what is the mind of the Spirit; because he maketh intercession for the saints, according to the will of God"* (Rom. viii. 27): that is to say, the Spirit demands only what is conformable to the will of God. The will of God is that we should be saved, and that we should become perfect: He, therefore, intercedes for all that is necessary for our perfection.

11. Why, then, should we be burthened with superfluous cares, and *weary ourselves in the multiplicity of our ways, without ever saying, let us rest in peace.* God himself invites us to cast all our care upon Him; and He complains in Isaiah, with ineffable goodness, that the soul had expended its powers and its treasures on a thousand external objects, when there was so little to do to attain all it need desire. *"Wherefore,"* saith God, *"do you spend money for that which is not bread; and your labor for that which satisfieth not? Hearken diligently unto me, and eat ye that which is good, and let your soul delight itself in fatness."* (Isa. lv. 2.)

Oh! did we but know the blessedness of thus hearkening to God, and how greatly the soul is strengthened by such a course! *"Be silent, O all flesh, before the Lord"* (Zech. ii. 13); all must cease as soon as He appears. But to engage us still farther to an abandonment without reservation, God assures us, by the same Prophet, that we need fear nothing, because he takes a very special care of us; *"Can a woman forget her sucking child, that she should not have compassion on the son of her womb? Yes, she may forget; yet will not I forget thee."* (Isa. xlix. 15.) O words full of consolation! Who after that will fear to abandon himself wholly to the guidance of God?

CHAPTER XXII.

1–6. Distinction between inward and outward acts; in this state the acts of the soul are inward, but habitual, continued, direct, lasting, deep, simple, unconscious, and resembling a gentle and perpetual sinking into the ocean of Divinity.

7, 8. A comparison.

9. How to act when we perceive no attraction.

Acts are distinguished into external and internal. *External* acts are those which appear outwardly, and bear relation to some sensible object, and have no moral character, except such as they derive from the principle from which they proceed. I intend here to speak only of *internal* acts, those energies of the soul, by which it turns internally towards some objects, and away from others.

2. If during my application to God, I should form a will to change the nature of my act, I should thereby withdraw myself from God and turn to created objects, and that in a greater or less degree according to the strength of the act: and if, when I

am turned towards the creature, I would return to God, I must necessarily form an act for that purpose; and the more perfect this act is, the more complete is the conversion.

Till conversion is perfected, many reiterated acts are necessary; for it is with some progressive, though with others it is instantaneous. My act, however, should consist in a continual turning to God, an exertion of every faculty and power of the soul purely for Him, agreeably to the instructions of the son of Sirach: *"Re-unite all the motions of thy heart in the holiness of God"* (Eccles. xxx. 24,); and to the example of David, *"I will keep my whole strength for thee,"* (Psalm lix. 9, vulg.) For we have strayed from our heart by sin, and it is our heart only that God requires: *"My son give me thine heart, and let thine eye observe my ways."* (Prov. xxiii. 26.) To give the heart to God, is to have the whole energy of the soul ever centering in Him, that we may be rendered conformable to his will. We must, therefore, continue invariably turned to God, from our first application to Him.

But the spirit being unstable, and the soul accustomed to turn to external objects, it is easily distracted. This evil, however, will be counteracted if, on perceiving the wandering, we, by a pure act of return to God, instantly replace ourselves in

Him; and this act subsists as long as the conversion lasts, by the powerful influence of a simple and unfeigned return to God.

3. As many reiterated acts form a habit, the soul contracts the habit of conversion; and that act which was before interrupted and distinct becomes habitual.

The soul should not, then, be perplexed about forming an act which already subsists, and which, indeed, it cannot attempt to form without very great difficulty; it even finds that it is withdrawn from its proper state, under pretence of seeking that which is in reality acquired, seeing the habit is already formed, and it is confirmed in habitual conversion and habitual love. It is seeking one act by the help of many, instead of continuing attached to God by one simple act alone.

We may remark, that at times we form with facility many *distant yet simple* acts; which shows that we have wandered, and that we re-enter our heart after having strayed from it; yet when we have re-entered, we should remain there in peace. We err, therefore, in supposing that we must not form acts; *we form them continually:* but let them be conformable to the degree of our spiritual advancement.

4. The great difficulty with most spiritual people arises from their not clearly comprehending this matter. Now, some acts are *transient and distinct*, others are *continued*, and again, some are *direct*, and others *reflective*. All cannot form the first, neither are all in a state suited to form the others. The first are adapted to those who have strayed, and who require a distinct exertion, proportioned to the extent of their deviation; if the latter be inconsiderable, an act of the most simple kind is sufficient.

5. By the *continued* act, I mean that whereby the soul is altogether turned toward God by a *direct* act, always subsisting, and which it does not renew unless it has been interrupted. The soul being thus turned, is in charity, and abides therein; *"and he that dwelleth in love, dwelleth in God."* (1 John iv. 16.) The soul then, is it were, exists and rests in the habitual act. It is, however, free from sloth; for there is still an *uninterrupted act subsisting,* which is a *sweet sinking into the Deity,* whose attraction becomes more and more powerful. Following this potent attraction, and dwelling in love and charity, the soul sinks continually deeper into that Love, maintaining an activity infinitely more powerful, vigorous, and effectual than that which served to accomplish its first return.

6. Now the soul that is thus *profoundly and vigorously active,* being wholly given up to God, does not perceive this act, because it is direct and not reflective. This is the reason why some, not expressing themselves properly, say, that they make no acts; but it is a mistake, for they were never more truly or nobly active; they should say, that *they did not distinguish their acts, and not that they did not act.* I grant that they do not act in themselves; but they are drawn, and they follow the attraction. Love is the weight which sinks them. As one falling into the sea, would sink from one depth to another to all eternity, if the sea were infinite, so they, without perceiving their descent, drop with inconceivable swiftness into the lowest deeps.

It is, then, improper to say that we do not make acts; all form acts, but the manner of their formation is not alike in all. The mistake arises from this, that all who know they should act, are desirous of acting *distinguishably and perceptibly;* but this cannot be: sensible acts are for beginners; there are others for those in a more advanced state. To stop in the former, which are weak and of little profit, is to declare ourselves of the latter; as to attempt the latter without having passed through the former, is a no less considerable error.

7. *"To everything there is a season"* (Eccles. iii. 1): every state has its commencement, its progress, and its consummation, and it is an unhappy error to stop in the beginning. There is no art but what has its progress; at first, we labor with toil, but at last we reap the fruit of our industry.

When the vessel is in port, the mariners are obliged to exert all their strength, that they may clear her thence, and put to sea; but they subsequently turn her with facility as they please. In like manner, while the soul remains in sin and the creature, many endeavors are requisite to effect its freedom; the cables which hold it must be loosed, and then by strong and vigorous efforts it gathers itself inward, pushes off gradually from the old port of Self, and, leaving that behind, proceeds to the interior, the haven so much desired.

8. When the vessel is thus started, as she advances on the sea, she leaves the shore behind; and the farther she departs from the land, the less labor is requisite in moving her forward. At length she begins to get gently under sail, and now proceeds so swiftly in her course, that the oars, which are become useless, are laid aside. How is the pilot now employed? he is content with spreading the sails and holding the rudder.

To spread the sails, is to lay ourselves before God in the prayer of simple exposition, to be moved by his Spirit; *to hold the rudder,* is to restrain our heart from wandering from the true course, recalling it gently, and guiding it steadily by the dictates of the Spirit of God, which gradually gains possession of the heart, just as the breeze by degrees fills the sails and impels the vessel. While the winds are fair, the pilot and the mariners rest from their labors. What progress do they not now secure, without the least fatigue! They make more way now in one hour, while they rest and leave the vessel to the wind, than they did in a length of time by all their former efforts; and even were they now to attempt using the oars, besides greatly fatiguing themselves, they would only retard the vessel by their useless exertions.

This is our proper course interiorly, and a short time will advance us by the divine impulsion farther than many reiterated acts of self-exertion. Whoever will try this path, will find it the easiest in the world.

9. If the wind be contrary and blow a storm, we must cast anchor in the sea, to hold the vessel. This anchor is simply trust in God and hope in his goodness, waiting patiently the calming of the tempest and the return of a favorable gale; thus did

David: *"I waited patiently for the Lord, and he inclined unto me, and heard my cry."* (Ps. xl. 1.) We must therefore be resigned to the Spirit of God, giving ourselves up wholly to his divine guidance.

CHAPTER XXIII.

1, 2. The barrenness of preaching, vice, error, heresies, and all sorts of evils arise from the fact that the people are not instructed in the prayer of the heart;

3–5. Although the way is surer, easier, and fitter for the simple minded.

6–8. Exhortation to pastors to set their flocks upon the practice of it, without employing them in studied forms and methodical devotion.

If all who labored for the conversion of others sought to reach them by the heart, introducing them immediately into prayer and the interior life, numberless and permanent conversions would ensue. On the contrary, few and transient fruits must attend that labor which is confined to outward matters, such as burdening the disciple with a thousand precepts for external exercises, instead of leading the soul to Christ by the occupation of the heart in Him.

If ministers were solicitous thus to instruct their parishioners, shepherds, while they watched their flocks, would have the spirit of the primitive Christians, and the husbandman at the plough maintain a blessed intercourse with his God; the manufacturer, while he exhausted his outward man with labor, would be renewed with inward strength; every species of vice would shortly disappear, and every parishioner become spiritually minded.

2. O when once the heart is gained, how easily is all the rest corrected! this is why God, above all things, requires the heart. By this means alone, we may extirpate the dreadful vices which so prevail among the lower orders, such as drunkenness, blasphemy, lewdness, enmity and theft. Jesus Christ would reign everywhere in peace, and the face of the church would be renewed throughout.

The decay of internal piety is unquestionably the source of the various errors that have appeared in the world; all would speedily be overthrown, were inward devotion re-established. Errors take possession of no soul, except such as are deficient in faith and prayer; and if, instead of engaging our wandering brethren in constant disputations, we would but teach them simply *to believe*, and diligently to *pray*, we should lead them sweetly to God.

O how inexpressibly great is the loss sustained by mankind from the neglect of the interior life! And what an account will those have to render who are entrusted with the care of souls, and have not discovered and communicated to their flock this hidden treasure!

3. Some excuse themselves by saying, that there is danger in this way, or that simple persons are incapable of comprehending the things of the Spirit. But the oracles of truth affirm the contrary: *"The Lord loveth those who walk simply."* (Prov. xii. 22, vulg.) But what danger can there be in walking in the only true way, which is Jesus Christ, giving ourselves up to Him, fixing our eye continually on Him, placing all our confidence in his grace, and tending with all the strength of our soul to his purest love?

4. The simple ones, so far from being incapable of this perfection, are, by their docility, innocence, and humility, peculiarly qualified for its attainment; and, as they are not accustomed to reasoning, they are less tenacious of their own opinions. Even from their want of learning, they submit more freely to the teachings of the divine

Spirit; whereas others, who are cramped and blinded by self-sufficiency, offer much greater resistance to the operations of grace.

We are told in Scripture that *"unto the simple, God giveth the understanding of his law"* (Psalm cxviii. 130, vulg.): and we are also assured, that God loves to communicate with them: *"The Lord careth for the simple; I was reduced to extremity and He saved me."* (Psalm cxvi. 6, cxv. 6, vulg.) Let spiritual fathers be careful how they prevent their little ones from coming to Christ; He himself said to his apostles, *"Suffer little children to come unto me, for of such is the kingdom of heaven."* (Matt. xix. 14.) It was the endeavor of the apostles to prevent children from going to our Lord, which occasioned this command.

5. Man frequently applies a remedy to the outward body, whilst the disease lies at the heart. The cause of our being so unsuccessful in reforming mankind, especially those of the lower classes, is our beginning with external matters; all our labors in this field, do but produce such fruit as endures not; but if the key of the interior be first given, the exterior would be naturally and easily reformed.

Now this is very easy. To teach man to seek God in his heart, to think of Him, to return to Him whenever he finds he has wandered from Him, and to do and suffer all things with a single eye to please Him, is leading the soul to the source of all grace, and causing it to find there everything necessary for sanctification.

6. I therefore beseech you all, O ye that have the care of souls, to put them at once into this way, which is Jesus Christ; nay, it is He himself that conjures you, by all the blood he has shed for those entrusted to you. *"Speak to the heart of Jerusalem!"* (Isa. xl. 2, vulg.) O ye dispensers of his grace! preachers of his word! ministers of his sacraments! establish his kingdom!—and that it may indeed be established, make Him ruler over the heart! For as it is the heart alone that can oppose his sovereignty, it is by the subjection of the heart that his sovereignty is most highly honored: *"Give glory to the holiness of God, and he shall become your sanctification."* (Isa. viii. 13, vulg.) Compose catechisms expressly to teach prayer, not by reasoning nor by method, for the simple are incapable of that; but to teach the prayer of the heart, not of the understanding; the prayer of God's Spirit, not of man's invention.

7. Alas! by directing them to pray in *elaborate forms*, and to be curiously critical therein, you create their chief obstacles. The children have been

led astray from the best of fathers, by your endeavoring to teach them too refined a language. Go, then, ye poor children, to your heavenly Father, speak to him in your natural language; rude and barbarous as it may be, it is not so to Him. A father is better pleased with an address which love and respect have made confused, because he sees that it proceeds from the heart, than he is by a dry and barren harangue, though never so elaborate. The simple and undisguised emotions of love are infinitely more expressive than all language, and all reasoning.

8. Men have desired to love Love by formal rules, and have thus lost much of that love. O how unnecessary is it to teach an art of loving! The language of love is barbarous to him that does not love, but perfectly natural to him that does; and there is no better way to learn how to love God, than to love him. The most ignorant often become the most perfect, because they proceed with more cordiality and simplicity. The Spirit of God needs none of our arrangements; when it pleases Him, He turns shepherds into Prophets, and, so far from excluding any from the temple of prayer, he throws wide the gates that all may enter; while wisdom is directed to cry aloud in the highways, *"Whoso is simple let him turn in hither"* (Prov. ix.

4); and to the fools she saith, *"Come eat of my bread, and drink of the wine which I have mingled."* (Prov. ix. 5.) And doth not Jesus Christ himself thank his Father for having *"hid these things from the wise and prudent, and revealed them unto babes?"* (Matt. xi. 25.)

CHAPTER XXIV.

On the passive way to Divine Union.

It is impossible to attain Divine Union, solely by the way of meditation, or of the affections, or by any devotion, no matter how illuminated. There are many reasons for this, the chief of which are those which follow.

1. According to Scripture, *"no man shall see God and live."* (Exod. xxxiii. 20.) Now all the exercises of discursive prayer, and even of *active contemplation,* regarded as an end, and not as a mere preparative to that which is passive, are still living exercises, by which we cannot see God; that is to say, be united with him. All that is of man and of his doing, be it never so noble, never so exalted, must first be destroyed.

St. John relates that there was silence in heaven. (Rev. viii. 1.) Now heaven represents the ground and centre of the soul, wherein all must be hushed to silence when the majesty of God appears. All the efforts, nay, the very existence, of self, must be destroyed; because nothing is opposite to God, but self, and all the malignity of man is in self-appropriation, as the source of its evil nature; insomuch that the purity of a soul increases in proportion as it loses this self-hood; and that which was a fault while the soul lived in self-appropriation, is no longer such, after it has acquired purity and innocence, by departing from that self-hood, which caused the dissimilitude between it and God.

2. To unite two things so opposite as the purity of God and the impurity of the creature, the simplicity of God and the multiplicity of man, much more is requisite than the efforts of the creature. Nothing less than an efficacious operation of the Almighty can ever accomplish this; for two things must have some relation or similarity before they can become one; as the impurity of dross cannot be united with the purity of gold.

3. What, then, does God do? He sends his own Wisdom before Him, as fire shall be sent upon the earth, to destroy by its activity all that is impure; and as nothing can resist the power of that fire, but it consumes everything, so this Wisdom destroys

all the impurities of the creature, in order to dispose it for divine union.

The impurity which is so fatal to union consists in *self-appropriation and activity. Self-appropriation;* because it is the source and fountain of all that defilement which can never be allied to essential purity; as the rays of the sun may shine, indeed, upon mire, but can never be united with it. *Activity;* for God being in an infinite stillness, the soul, in order to be united to Him, must participate of his stillness, else the contrariety between stillness and activity would prevent assimilation.

Therefore, the soul can never arrive at divine union but in the rest of its will; nor can it ever become one with God, but by being re-established in central rest and in the purity of its first creation.

4. God purifies the soul by his Wisdom, as refiners do metals in the furnace. Gold cannot be purified but by fire, which gradually consumes all that is earthy and foreign, and separates it from the metal. It is not sufficient to fit it for use that the earthy part should be changed into gold; it must then be melted and dissolved by the force of fire, to separate from the mass every drossy or alien particle; and must be again and again cast into the

furnace, until it has lost every trace of pollution, and every possibility of being farther purified.

The goldsmith cannot now discover any adulterate mixture, because of its perfect purity and simplicity. The fire no longer touches it; and were it to remain an age in the furnace, its spotlessness would not be increased, nor its substance diminished. It is then fit for the most exquisite workmanship, and if, thereafter, this gold seem obscured or defiled, it is nothing more than an accidental impurity occasioned by the contact of some foreign body, and is only superficial; it is no hinderance to its employment, and is widely different from its former debasement, which was hidden in the ground of its nature, and, as it were, identified with it. Those, however, who are uninstructed, beholding the pure gold sullied by some external pollution, would be disposed to prefer an impure and gross metal, that appeared superficially bright and polished.[8]

---

[8] "God knows that (in speaking of the superficial impurity) I had only reference to certain defects which are exterior and entirely natural, and which are left by God in the greatest saints to keep them from pride, and the sight of men, who judge only from the outward appearance, to preserve them from corruption, and hide them in the secret of his presence. (Ps. xxxi. 20.) At the time I wrote, I had heard no mention of the perversions subsequently spoken of that those in union with God might sin and yet remain united to Him, and, as

5. Farther, the pure and the impure gold are not mingled; before they can be united, they must be equally refined; the goldsmith cannot mix dross and gold. What will he do, then? He will purge out the dross with fire, so that the inferior may become as pure as the other, and then they may be united. This is what St. Paul means, when he declares that "*the fire shall try every man's work of what sort it is*" (1 Cor. iii 3); he adds, *"If any man's work be burnt, he shall suffer loss, but he himself shall be saved, yet so as by fire."* He here intimates, that there are works so degraded by impure mixtures, that though the mercy of God accepts them, yet they must pass through the fire, to be purged from self; and it is in this sense that God is said to examine and judge our righteousness, because that by the deeds of the law there shall no flesh be justified; but by the righteousness of God, which is by faith in Jesus Christ. (Rom. iii. 20, etc.)

6. Thus we may see that the divine justice and wisdom, like a pitiless and devouring fire, must destroy all that is earthly, sensual, and carnal, and all self-activity, before the soul can be united to its God. Now, this can never be accomplished by the

---

such an idea had not once occurred to me, I never imagined that it was possible for any one to draw such inferences from a simple illustration."-Mad. Guyon, Courte Apologie, etc.

industry of the creature; on the contrary, he always submits to it with reluctance; because, as I have said, he is so enarmored of self, and so fearful of its destruction, that did not God act upon him powerfully and with authority, he would never consent.

7. It may, perhaps, be objected here, that as God never robs man of his free will, he can always resist the divine operations; and that I therefore err in saying *God acts absolutely, and without the consent of man.*

Let me, however, explain. By man's giving a *passive consent,* God, without usurpation, may assume full power and an entire guidance; for having, in the beginning of his conversion, made an unreserved surrender of himself to all that God wills of him or by him, he thereby gave an active consent to whatever God might afterwards require. But when God begins to burn, destroy, and purify, the soul does not perceive that these operations are intended for its good, but rather supposes the contrary; and, as the gold at first seems rather to blacken than brighten in the fire, so it conceives that its purity is lost; insomuch, that if an *active and explicit* consent were then required, the soul could scarcely give it, nay would often withhold it. All it does is to remain firm in its passive consent, enduring as patiently as possible all these divine operations, which it is neither able nor desirous to obstruct.

8. In this manner, therefore, the soul is purified from all its self-originated, distinct, perceptible, and multiplied operations, which constitute a great dissimilitude between it and God; it is rendered by degrees *conform,* and then *uniform;* and the passive capacity of the creature is elevated, ennobled, and enlarged, though in a secret and hidden manner, hence called mystical; but in all these operations the soul must concur passively. It is true, indeed, that in the beginning its activity is requisite; from which, however, as the divine operations become stronger, it must gradually cease; yielding itself up to the impulse of the divine Spirit, till it is wholly absorbed in Him. But this is a process which lasts a long time.

9. We do not, then, say, as some have supposed, that there is no need of activity; since, on the contrary, it is the gate; at which, however, we should not always tarry, since we ought to tend towards ultimate perfection, which is impracticable except the first helps are laid aside; for however necessary they may have been at the entrance of the road, they afterwards become greatly detrimental to those who adhere to them

obstinately, preventing them from ever attaining the end. This made St. Paul say, *"Forgetting those things which are behind, and reaching forth to those which are before, I press toward the mark, for the prize of the high calling of God in Christ Jesus."* (Phil. iii. 13.)

Would you not say that he had lost his senses, who, having undertaken a journey, should fix his abode at the first inn, because he had been told that many travellers had come that way, that some had lodged there, and that the masters of the house dwelt there? All that we wish, then, is, that souls would press toward the end, taking the shortest and easiest road, and not stopping at the first stage. Let them follow the counsel and example of St. Paul, and suffer themselves to be led by the Spirit of God, (Rom. viii. 14,) which will infallibly conduct them to the end of their creation, the enjoyment of God.

10. But while we confess that the enjoyment of God is the end for which alone we were created, and that every soul that does not attain divine union and the purity of its creation in this life, can only be saved as by fire, how strange it is, that we should dread and avoid the process; as if that could be the cause of evil and imperfection in the present

life, which is to produce the perfection of glory in the life to come.

11. None can be ignorant that God is the Supreme Good; that essential blessedness consists in union with Him; that the saints differ in glory, according as the union is more or less perfect; and that the soul cannot attain this union by the mere activity of its own powers, since God communicates Himself to the soul, in proportion as its passive capacity is great, noble and extensive. We can only be united to God in simplicity and passivity, and as this union is beatitude itself, the way that leads us in this passivity cannot be evil, but must be the most free from danger, and the best.

12. This way is not dangerous. Would Jesus Christ have made this the most perfect and necessary of all ways, had it been so? No! all can travel it; and as all are called to happiness, all are likewise called to the enjoyment of God, both in this life and the next, for that alone is happiness. I say the enjoyment of God himself, and not of his gifts; these latter do not constitute essential beatitude, as they cannot fully content the soul; it is so noble and so great, that the most exalted gifts of God cannot make it happy, unless the Giver also bestows Himself. Now the whole desire of the Divine Being is to give Himself to every creature,

according to the capacity with which it is endowed; and yet, alas! how reluctantly man suffers himself to be drawn to God! how fearful is he to prepare for divine union!

13. Some say, that we *must not place ourselves in this state.* I grant it; but I say also, that no creature could ever do it; since it would not be possible for any, by all their own efforts, to unite themselves to God; it is He alone must do it. It is altogether idle, then, to exclaim against those who are self-united, as such a thing cannot be.

They say again, that *some may feign to have attained this state.* None can any more feign this, than the wretch who is on the point of perishing with hunger can, for any length of time at least, feign to be full and satisfied. Some wish or word, some sigh or sign, will inevitably escape him, and betray that he is far from being satisfied.

Since then none can attain this end by their own labor, we do not pretend to introduce any into it, but *only to point out the way that leads to it:* beseeching all not *to become attached to the accommodations on the road, external practices, which must all be left behind when the signal is given.* The experienced instructor knows this, points to the water of life, and lends his aid to obtain it. Would it not be an unjustifiable cruelty to show a spring to a thirsty man, then bind him so that he could not reach it, and suffer him to die of thirst?

14. This is just what is done every day. Let us all agree in the way, as we all agree in the end, which is evident and incontrovertible. The way has its beginning, process, and termination; and the nearer we approach the consummation, the farther is the beginning behind us; it is only by leaving the one, that we can arrive at the other. You cannot get from the entrance to a distant place, without passing over the intermediate space, and, if the end be good, holy, and necessary, and the entrance also good, why should the necessary passage, the direct road leading from the one to the other, be evil?

O the blindness of the greater part of mankind, who pride themselves on science and wisdom! How true is it, O my God, *that thou hast hid these things from the wise and prudent, and hast revealed them unto babes!*

ABOUT CROSSREACH PUBLICATIONS

 Thank you for choosing CrossReach Publications.

Trust. Inspiration. Hope.

These three words sum up the philosophy of why CrossReach Publications exist. You want solid Christian books from respected and acknowledged Christian writers from yesteryear. We want to provide them for you.

Not only do you get the works of the most well-known men and women of Christendom, we have also brought back many lesser-known works from some of the giants from Church history, as well as hidden gems from less popular, and even almost forgotten authors that deserve to be heard again.

Not only that, our editions are also high quality. We spend time editing and formatting and looking over our manuscripts before publishing. Some small publishers of classic works publish sloppy, almost illegible reproductions of these works. This will not do. We aspire to excellence and we believe it shows in our editions. We cannot guarantee perfection, but we'll try. And we do this at a cost that is right for you.

If you have any questions or comments about our publications contact us:

ContactUs@CrossReach.net
https://www.CrossReach.store

Don't forget you can follow us on Facebook and Twitter, (addresses are on the copyright page above) to keep up to date on our newest titles and deals.

BESTSELLING TITLES FROM CROSSREACH[1]

God Still Speaks
A. W. Tozer
$6.99
https://amazon.com/dp/154980894X

Tozer is as popular today as when he was living on the earth. He is respected right across the spectrum of Christianity, in circles that would disagree sharply with him doctrinally. Why is this? A. W. Tozer was a man who knew the voice of God. He shared this experience with every true child of God. With all those who are called by the grace of God to share in the mystical union that is possible with Him through His Son Jesus.

Tozer fought against much dryness and formality in his day. Considered a mighty man of God by most Evangelicals today, he was unconventional in his approach to spirituality and had no qualms about consulting everyone from Catholic Saints to German

---

[1] Most of our eBooks cost between $0.99 and $1.99. Most of our paperbacks cost $7.99 or less. Click on the title of each to be brought to the eBook edition or if this is a paperback, then copy the address into your internet browser. Buy from CrossReach Publications for quality and price. We have a full selection of titles in print and eBook, available on Amazon and a growing selection of other online stores. You can see our full selection just by searching for CrossReach Publications in the search bar of these stores! Please note also, that the additional pages these advertisement make up come at no extra cost to you the reader. You have paid only for the work itself.

Protestant mystics for inspiration on how to experience God more fully.

Tozer, just like his Master, doesn't fit neatly into our theological boxes. He was a man after God's own heart and was willing to break the rules (man-made ones that is) to get there.

Here are two writings by Tozer that touch on the heart of this goal. Revelation is Not Enough and The Speaking Voice. A bonus chapter The Menace of the Religious Movie is included.

This is meat to sink your spiritual teeth into. Tozer's writings will show you the way to satisfy your spiritual hunger.

A. W. TOZER
HOW TO BE
Filled
WITH
THE
Holy Spirit

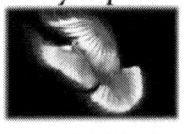

CrossReach Publications

How to Be Filled with the Holy Spirit

A. W. Tozer

$6.99

https://amazon.com/dp/1549774190

Before we deal with the question of how to be filled with the Holy Spirit, there are some matters which first have to be settled. As believers you have to get them out of the way, and right here is where the difficulty arises. I have been afraid that my listeners might have gotten the idea somewhere that I had a how-to-be-filled-with-the-Spirit-in-five-easy-lessons doctrine, which I could give you. If you can have any such vague ideas as that, I can only stand before you and say, "I am sorry"; because it isn't true; I can't give you such a course. There are some things, I say, that you have to get out of the way, settled.

The 400 Silent Years
H. A. Ironside
$7.50
https://amazon.com/dp/1549816039

Fully illustrated. Includes all of the drawings from the original edition.

What is the history between the Old and New Testaments? Most people are not even aware there is such a gap. But there is. A 400 year gap.

When the Old Testament leaves off the Jews have just returned back from Babylonian captivity and the Persian Empire is in full swing. When Jesus enters the scene it is 400 years later. The Persians are long gone, the Greeks have had their time and now the Romans rule to roost.

So what happened? Do we have any writings from this time? Could understanding this period of time help us understand the New Testament, the world of Jesus and the Apostles? The answer is yes.

This exciting book by well-known author H. A. Ironside lifts the veil from this vital period of Jewish history and helps piece together the events that brought them from Malachi to Matthew.

This book will be of interested to students of Biblical, Ancient Near Eastern, Greek and Roman history as well as all those who desire to know and understand the Bible for fully.

Christianity and Liberalism
J. Gresham Machen

The purpose of this book is not to decide the religious issue of the present day, but merely to present the issue as sharply and clearly as possible, in order that the reader may be aided in deciding it for himself. Presenting an issue sharply is indeed by no means a popular business at the present time; there are many who prefer to fight their intellectual battles in what Dr. Francis L. Patton has aptly called a "condition of low visibility." Clear-cut definition of terms in religious matters, bold facing of the logical implications of religious views, is by many persons regarded as an impious proceeding. May it not discourage contribution to mission boards? May it not hinder the progress of consolidation, and produce a poor showing in columns of Church statistics? But with such persons we cannot possibly bring ourselves to agree. Light may seem at times to be an impertinent intruder, but it is always beneficial in the end. The type of religion which rejoices in the pious sound of traditional phrases, regardless of their meanings, or shrinks from "controversial" matters, will never stand amid the shocks of life. In the sphere of religion, as in other spheres, the things about which men are agreed are apt to be the things that are least worth holding; the really important things are the things about which men will fight.

The Two Babylons
Alexander Hislop
$7.99
https://amazon.com/dp/1549771191

Fully Illustrated High Res. Images. Complete and Unabridged.

Expanded Seventh Edition. This is the first and only seventh edition available in a modern digital edition. Nothing is left out! New material not found in the first six editions!!! Available in eBook and paperback edition exclusively from CrossReach Publications.

"In his work on "The Two Babylons" Dr. Hislop has proven conclusively that all the idolatrous systems of the nations had their origin in what was founded by that mighty Rebel, the beginning of whose kingdom was Babel (Gen. 10:10)."—A. W. Pink, The Antichrist (1923)

There is this great difference between the works of men and the works of God, that the same minute and searching investigation, which displays the defects and imperfections of the one, brings out also the beauties of the other. If the most finely polished needle on which the art of man has been expended be subjected to a microscope, many inequalities, much roughness and clumsiness, will be seen. But if the microscope be brought to bear on the flowers of the field, no such result appears. Instead of their beauty diminishing, new beauties and still more delicate, that have escaped the naked eye, are forthwith discovered; beauties that make us appreciate, in a way which otherwise we could have had little conception of, the full force of the Lord's saying, "Consider the lilies of the field, how they grow;

they toil not, neither do they spin: and yet I say unto you, That even Solomon, in all his glory, was not arrayed like one of these." The same law appears also in comparing the Word of God and the most finished productions of men. There are spots and blemishes in the most admired productions of human genius. But the more the Scriptures are searched, the more minutely they are studied, the more their perfection appears; new beauties are brought into light every day; and the discoveries of science, the researches of the learned, and the labours of infidels, all alike conspire to illustrate the wonderful harmony of all the parts, and the Divine beauty that clothes the whole. If this be the case with Scripture in general, it is especially the case with prophetic Scripture. As every spoke in the wheel of Providence revolves, the prophetic symbols start into still more bold and beautiful relief. This is very strikingly the case with the prophetic language that forms the groundwork and corner-stone of the present work. There never has been any difficulty in the mind of any enlightened Protestant in identifying the woman "sitting on seven mountains," and having on her forehead the name written, "Mystery, Babylon the Great," with the Roman apostacy.

WHAT WE ARE IN CHRIST

What We Are In Christ
E. W. Kenyon
$5.99
https://amazon.com/dp/1549823094

I was surprised to find that the expressions "in Christ," "in whom," and "in Him" occur more than 130 times in the New Testament. This is the heart of the Revelation of Redemption given to Paul. Here is the secret of faith—faith that conquers, faith that moves mountains. Here is the secret of the Spirit's guiding us into all reality. The heart craves intimacy with the Lord Jesus and with the Father. This craving can now be satisfied.

Ephesians 1:7: "In whom we have our redemption through his blood, the remission of our trespasses according to the riches of his grace."

It is not a beggarly Redemption, but a real liberty in Christ that we have now. It is a Redemption by the God Who could say, "Let there be lights in the firmament of heaven," and cause the whole starry heavens to leap into being in a single instant. It is Omnipotence beyond human reason. This is where philosophy has never left a footprint.

The Complete Wycliffe Bible: Old Testament, New Testament & Apocrypha: Text Edition
$18.99

https://amazon.com/dp/154978692X

In making this edition of Wycliffe's monumental work the Publisher has had to make a number of decisions that affect the final outcome of the work. Some of these decisions may be welcomed by the reading public and some perhaps not. All of the decisions were made with the reader in mind. Our intention was to produce an edition of Wycliffe's Bible translation that was reasonably priced and to do this it must be in one volume. This has meant choosing a large paper format. Other smaller sized editions are over 800 pages. We chose a larger paper size that results in around 250 pages less. We chose a font that is recognized as easily readable at smaller sizes. Adobe Garamond, 10 pt. was selected. We have tested it and have not found it to be an uncomfortable reading size. If you have reasonable eyesight, you will not need a magnifying glass, as has been reportedly needed for other modern reprints. We hope you like it. Some will complain that we have not inserted indents and paragraphing. Again, this is a massive volume and we have tried to produce a book that is within one volume so that it is commercially viable for us and you the reader. It has also meant not including any of the introductions by Wycliffe, Jerome and others, or notes that were a part of the original. Hence the subtitle "Text Edition". We understand this will not be to everyone's liking, but we are limited, by the printer, to how many pages our books can be. At the size we chose we are almost at capacity. At a smaller size we could have done over 800 pages, but we still would have had to cram the same amount of text in. So the problem would be the same. The only way around this problem would have been to produce two large volumes and at this time we do question the viability of such an undertaking. However, if it is clear that there is a great demand for it, we may bring out a new two volume edition with that additional text. This work was first produced in the late Middle Ages. The language is therefore extremely archaic. So much so that some of the letters have evolved and changed since then. This edition contains all modern letters, but does not contain modern spelling. It is therefore, not a "Modern Edition" in this sense. The yogh for example has been replaced as necessary. Purists will complain, but we hope for the average reader this will not present much of a problem. It will hopefully give the reader a text as close to the original yet still possible to be read and, with a little work, understood.

How to Prepare Sermons
William Evans
$7.99
https://amazon.com/dp/154981785X

HOW TO PREPARE
SERMONS
William Evans

This volume is not an attempt to present a complete and exhaustive treatment on Homiletics—the science and art of preaching, for there are already on the market larger and more comprehensive works on the subject. This book is prepared not only for theological students but also to supply the need of such as find themselves denied the privileges of a regular ministerial training, but who, nevertheless, feel themselves called upon to preach or proclaim the gospel of the Lord Jesus Christ. Indeed the lectures herein printed are in substance the same as delivered to young men and women preparing themselves for Christian service in a Bible training school. This fact accounts for their conversational style, which the author has not deemed wise to change. Christian laymen, even though not preachers in the accepted sense of that term, desiring to be able to prepare brief gospel addresses and Bible readings, will find the help they need in this volume. Those seeking help in the preparation of "talks" for young peoples' societies, conventions, leagues, etc., may receive hints and suggestions in this work. The book contains theory and practice. Part One deals with the method of constructing various kinds of sermons and Bible addresses. Part Two is composed of outlines illustrating Part One. The closing chapter on "Illustrations and Their Use" has been found so helpful wherever delivered that it is thought advisable to give it a place in this volume.

A Medicine Chest for Christian Practitioners
Clarence Larkin
$4.99
https://amazon.com/dp/1520411316

This booklet is designed to give tools for Christian service. Clarence Larkin was born October 28, 1850, in Chester, Delaware County, Pennsylvania. He was converted to Christ at the age of 19. He was a mechanical engineer, teacher and manufacturer by trade. In 1884, at the age of 34, he became an ordained Baptist minister. His first pastorate was at Kennett Square, Pennsylvania; his second was at Fox Chase, Pennsylvania, where he remained for 20 years. He was not a premillennialist at the time of his ordination, but his study of the Scriptures, with the help of some books that fell into his hands, led him to adopt the premillennialist position. He began to make large wall charts, which he titled, "Prophetic Truth," for use in the pulpit. These led to his being invited to teach, in connection with his pastoral work, in two Bible institutes. During this time he published a number of prophetical charts, which were widely circulated. He spent three years of his life designing and drawing the charts and preparing the text for his most noteworthy book "Dispensational Truth." Because it had a large and wide circulation in this and other lands, the first edition was soon exhausted. It was followed by a second edition, and then, realizing that the book was of permanent value, Larkin revised it and expanded it, printing it in its present form. Larkin followed this masterpiece with other books. During the last five years of his life, the demand for Larkin's books made it necessary for him to give up the pastorate and devote his full time to writing. He went to be with the Lord on January 24, 1924.—The Christian Worker's Outfit

CLAIMING OUR RIGHTS

Claiming Our Rights
E. W. Kenyon
$7.99
www.amazon.com/dp/1549815148

There is no excuse for the spiritual weakness and poverty of the Family of God when the wealth of Grace and Love of our great Father with His power and wisdom are all at our disposal. We are not coming to the Father as a tramp coming to the door begging for food; we come as sons not only claiming our legal rights but claiming the natural rights of a child that is begotten in love. No one can hinder us or question our right of approach to our Father.

Satan has Legal Rights over the sinner that God cannot dispute or challenge. He can sell them as slaves; he owns them, body, soul and spirit. But the moment we are born again... receive Eternal Life, the nature of God,—his legal dominion ends.

Christ is the Legal Head of the New Creation, or Family of God, and all the Authority that was given Him, He has given us: (Matthew 28:18), "All authority in heaven," the seat of authority, and "on earth," the place of execution of authority. He is "head over all things," the highest authority in the Universe, for the benefit of the Church which is His body.

The Person and Work of the Holy Spirit
R. A. Torrey
$5.85
www.amazon.com/dp/1549821490

Before one can correctly understand the work of the Holy Spirit, he must first of all know the Spirit Himself. A frequent source of error and fanaticism about the work of the Holy Spirit is the attempt to study and understand His work without first of all coming to know Him as a Person.

It is of the highest importance from the standpoint of worship that we decide whether the Holy Spirit is a Divine Person, worthy to receive our adoration, our faith, our love, and our entire surrender to Himself, or whether it is simply an influence emanating from God or a power or an illumination that God imparts to us. If the Holy Spirit is a person, and a Divine Person, and we do not know Him as such, then we are robbing a Divine Being of the worship and the faith and the love and the surrender to Himself which are His due.

Home Geography for the Primary Grades
C. C. Long
$7.95
https://amazon.com/dp/1518780660

A popular homeschooling resource for many generations now. Geography may be divided into the geography of the home and the geography of the world at large. A knowledge of the home must be obtained by direct observation; of the rest of the world, through the imagination assisted by information. Ideas acquired by direct observation form a basis for imagining those things which are distant and unknown. The first work, then, in geographical instruction, is to study that small part of the earth's surface lying just at our doors. All around are illustrations of lake and river, upland and lowland, slope and valley. These forms must be actually observed by the pupil, mental pictures obtained, in order that he may be enabled to build up in his mind other mental pictures of similar unseen forms. The hill that he climbs each day may, by an appeal to his imagination, represent to him the lofty Andes or the Alps. From the meadow, or the bit of level land near the door, may be developed a notion of plain and prairie. The little stream that flows past the schoolhouse door, or even one formed by the sudden shower, may speak to him of the Mississippi, the Amazon, or the Rhine. Similarly, the idea of sea or ocean may be deduced from that of pond or lake. Thus, after the pupil has acquired elementary ideas by actual perception, the imagination can use them in constructing, on a larger scale, mental pictures of similar objects outside the bounds of his own experience and observation.

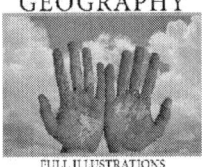

Elementary Geography
Charlotte Mason
$8.99
https://amazon.com/dp/1549774859

This little book is confined to very simple "reading lessons upon the Form and Motions of the Earth, the Points of the Compass, the Meaning of a Map: Definitions."
It is hoped that these reading lessons may afford intelligent teaching, even in the hands of a young teacher.
Children should go through the book twice, and should, after the second reading, be able to answer any of the questions from memory.

Manufactured by Amazon.ca
Bolton, ON